PAUL

MAY ALL YOUR
TREASURES BE A
WEALTH OF VALUES,
BELIEFS & TRADITI?

All The Best

THE
MAGIC
OF MONEY

21 *ACTION* STRATEGIES TO MAKE MONEY **WORK** FOR YOU

RICH GAINES

ISBN: 978 0 692 49207 9

ACKNOWLEDGMENTS

Book writing takes a community of people to complete.

I want to acknowledge those people who have inspired me along the way and provided me with the desire to do the hard work of writing this book. First and foremost are the mentors who helped me to achieve a higher purpose in life by helping others. Specifically Clinton Swaine of Frontier Trainings. The experiences and lessons I received in speaking, business building, and personal growth provided me with a river of confidence and transformation in the value of what I have to offer others from all of my background, education, and experience. Also Bob Donnell of Next Level Entrepreneur Association, who through his mix of generosity and results-oriented support gave me the comfort that with the mindset of certainty, each step of doing will move me toward my ultimate destination.

I want to acknowledge the creative marketing and branding experts who helped me position my message of wealth success in a way that it will resonate, transform, and inspire. I want to acknowledge the people responsible in preparing this book for print. Friends, copywriters, proofreaders and others who provided feedback and insight into the various ideas and chapters of the book.

Lastly, accomplishments are next to impossible without the love of family and good friends. Nothing in life is more important than family and friends, because no matter how bad things might seem, at the end of the day, only family and good friends will be there for you. Thank you to my wife Shelley, who has stood by me all these years. Thank you to my children Jordan and Taylor, who are amazing adults with integrity and purpose. Thank you to my parents, who as of this writing are still going strong in their late 80s and 90s. And thank you to my brothers, who have provided me with all kinds of stories from our years of growing up together.

OTHER BOOKS BY RICH GAINES

Generations
My Family Treasures
Preserving the Story, History and Facts of My Family.

Business Strengtheners
Key Strategies to Move from Survival
to Security to Affluence.

To order either of these books, please visit
www.mindmoneystrategy.com or
www.legacy-legal.com

CONTENTS

Preface... 1

About Rich Gaines.. 3

Introduction.. 7

Action Strategy 1: Master Fine Distinctions............ 13

Action Strategy 2: Master Ego and Find Your True Self... 25

Action Strategy 3: It's All in Your Mind.................. 31

Action Strategy 4: Mind Clogs.............................. 47

Action Strategy 5: Unclog with Clog Busters........... 65

Action Strategy 6: Lifestyle Treasure Map.............. 75

Action Strategy 7: Clarity Is Lucky #7.................... 77

Action Strategy 8: Doubt? What Doubt?
   I Have a Business Plan...................................... 87

Action Strategy 9: The 30-Second Impression 107

Action Strategy 10: Build a Brick House.............. 115

Action Strategy 11: Three Ways to Make Money.... 121

Action Strategy 12: Stay Out of the Poorhouse 125

Action Strategy 13: Master Budget, Master You 129

Action Strategy 14: Top Ten List.......................... 135

Action Strategy 15: Pay Yourself First.................. 159

Action Strategy 16: The Fallacy of the Rule of 72 163

Action Strategy 17: Cash Flow Is King 167

Action Strategy 18: Beware the Tax Demons 171

Action Strategy 19: Find Your Tax Angels 175

Action Strategy 20: Good Is the Enemy of Great ... 181

Action Strategy 21: Nourish Legacy

Through Leadership 185

Appendix 1: Income and Expense Compass 193

Appendix 2: Rule of 72 Simple Calculation 197

Appendix 3: Rule of 72 Adding Money Each Year ... 198

PREFACE

Unless you win the lottery or are extremely lucky, the process of making money and keeping money takes time and hard work. They say it takes ten years to become an overnight success. Roger Federer winning 17 Grand Slams in tennis. Barry Bonds setting a new home run record. It didn't happen overnight. It took a lifetime of training.

I am not suggesting you need a lifetime of training. I am suggesting that by reading and following the 21 simple strategies in this book, you can accelerate the learning curve to overcoming barriers, building wealth, and nourishing a legacy for generations.

In my 30 years of experience as a tax attorney and wealth strategist I have been a catalyst for businesses and families to clearly define their success, overcome barriers, make money, and keep money. I have found that when people fail to take the right steps and the right actions in planning wealth, the business or family can get ripped apart, brothers and sisters can stop talking, and money that could be invested gets wasted on frivolous lawsuits. For these reasons, as well as overcoming my own limiting beliefs around money, I developed *The Magic of Money*. In *The Magic of Money*, I make you aware of minefields that can blow up your plans, show you what to watch out for, point out weak links, and provide you with strategies to make money and keep money.

One of the unique features of *The Magic of Money* is that it focuses on the idea that wealth has a sequence, an order. If you take the right actions at the right time and in the right order, wealth—not only in money, but in values, beliefs, and traditions—will follow. If you take actions out of order, you can make building wealth much more difficult. Do you find yourself doing the same things over and over again and expecting a different result? That is the classic definition of insanity. Do you want a different result? *The Magic of Money* can provide it for you. In the end, whether we like it or not, we will all leave a legacy. The only question is whether it will be a legacy of your own choosing and one that will make you proud.

With this book you will receive valuable information, quick and easy strategies that take you step by step through the process and sequence of building wealth and nourishing legacy.

ABOUT RICH GAINES

Rich Gaines is a leading legal and tax expert. He supports businesses and families in planning their wealth. His other publications include **Generations:** *My Family Treasures; Preserving the Story, History and Facts of My Family*, and **Business Strengtheners***: Key Strategies to Move from Survival to Security to Affluence.*

Rich pursued a legal education, graduating from Southwestern University School of Law in 1983, and went on to complete the highest level of training in tax law at Denver University School of Law, where he received a Master of Laws in Taxation in 1984.

Rich started his career working for a national CPA firm and then continued as an associate attorney in midsize law firms, both in the Inland Empire and San Diego. His work concentrated on multimillion-dollar business and real estate transactions with an emphasis on tax strategies and tactics. He has prepared thousands of estate and tax plans for clients seeking to build wealth, to protect it, and to prepare new generations to receive wealth.

Rich's clients have ranged from people who have modest wealth to high–net worth family businesses seeking to protect their wealth for generations. Rich utilizes proven strategies in business, money, estate and tax law to accomplish the purpose, vision, and goals of the clientele he serves. *The Magic of Money* is an outgrowth of Rich's desire and goal to distill his years of experience into simple and easy-to-follow strategies.

In 2010, Rich formed Legacy Legal, Inc., a boutique law firm in North San Diego County whose vision is to tap into the tremendous potential in businesses and families to build wealth. The mission of the firm is to change the way people think and talk about wealth, not only in money, but in values, beliefs, and traditions. In his industry, Rich is doing something no one else is doing. He hosts seminars where participants engage and interact through exercises and games, which cultivates learning in a fun environment.

Rich has served as head of the tax section for the North County Bar Association, Treasurer and Board of Director of Jewish Family Services, a prominent charitable organization in San Diego, participated in the fund-raising branch of the Motino Family YMCA in Oceanside and TERI, Inc. He was president of the local chapter of an international networking organization, chair of a Business Legacy Mentoring Group, and chair of the San Diego Speaker's Bureau of Toastmasters International. He has been a featured guest on KFMB and ESPN Radio. Over the last 15 years, Rich has spoken to a variety of groups in San Diego, including Rotary, Kiwanis, Professional Business Organizers, attorneys, Toastmasters, CPAs, and more. He also has conducted public seminars, including "Speak Like A Pro," "Minefields of Wills and Trusts," and "Master Self-Master Wealth."

Rich lives in Carlsbad, California, with his wife, and they have twins. His passions include tennis, where he has won numerous awards in singles and doubles and was once ranked number one in his division in San Diego County in doubles; and skiing, which he has done all his life. He was fortunate to be able to travel into the Canadian Rockies on a helicopter ski trip, a truly life-changing experience. Rich has a real wealth commitment. His name, Rich Gaines, his advanced training in tax law, his more than 30-year career as a tax attorney, and his twins, Jordan and Taylor, who were born on April 15. Can't make that up.

INTRODUCTION

A JOURNEY OF A THOUSAND MILES STARTS WITH THE FIRST STEP

Every day I sat in my office drafting estate plans, wills, and trusts, and representing people with tax problems. I formed business entities and helped business owners save money from the big arms of Uncle Sam. I was planning for their future, but after 23 years, I peered out the window one day and realized there had to be something better, something greater, something bigger in life. I needed to find a way to take the knowledge and experience I had and create a greater value than simply meeting people who would spend time in my office. I saw how many people's plans, once completed, simply sat on a shelf collecting dust, and I wanted to find more value and meaning for people than building, protecting, and preserving money for money's sake.

As I approached age 50, I knew what people valued most. What was it that I found? It wasn't money. It was wealth. Wealth means values, beliefs, traditions, and wisdom. When our lives have meaning and purpose, we have the ability to make a difference and impact the world with greater value. Meaning and purpose is not enough by itself. We also have to put in the hard work of bridging the gap between our future fortunes and everyday present actions. All these actions are designed for your success.

This book is the culmination of that effort. *The Magic of Money* is just that. It is a guide containing 21 actions that can change the way you think and talk about wealth. When you are ready to change your approach to your money, your business, and maybe even your life, you are ready for *The Magic of Money*.

IT'S GO TIME. LET'S ROCK AND ROLL!

Shannon K. Parish

Like the old joke, how do you eat an elephant? ... One bite at a time. Something that looms so large—climbing a mountain, running a marathon, getting on stage in front of a thousand-person audience—starts small. Every journey starts with a first step. *The Magic of Money* is like eating an elephant. It is a journey. Each strategy, each step brings you closer to the lifestyle you have imagined. With each step can come a great sense of immediate gratification. What is great about this journey is that every time I think I have discovered the perfect combination for wealth, happiness, and success, I find that each new life experience, each new day just evolves my perspective and reveals more treasures this world can hold for us. *The Magic of Money* contains 21 simple action steps that can and should become a part of a wealth-building journey. The journey no doubt will have high points and low points. The journey will have obstacles along the way, to be sure. However, this journey will open up incredible opportunities and a chance to realize hopes and dreams that come with success at every step of the way.

The 21 action strategies to building wealth contain common principles and rules that apply to all of us. Yet, people still bring their own unique and different culture, background, perspectives, experiences, and choices in applying the principles and rules. No one person's journey is right, wrong, good, bad, better, or worse. Each person has the opportunity to determine and define how much is just right for them.

The 21 action strategies to building wealth contain some core building blocks. Each one stands alone, yet all are very interdependent. Like life, sometimes it may be easy to accelerate forward, while other times it may feel like being stuck in a fog, and sometimes one might have to go backward before pressing on. Each action strategy has principles and rules that, if followed, can lead to great success. The action strategies are designed to be sequential. Follow the sequence, and your foundations will be strong. Take the action strategies out of order, and it may be tougher to create the solid structure of building wealth and nourishing legacy. This having been said, every person is different and may find focusing on certain parts of the sequence to be more immediately valuable than others. However, without success in one area, it may be difficult to find success in another area. For example, I talk about the right mindset. If your mindset isn't right and you jump ahead, you may find disaster looming around the corner and not know it. It's hard to think about protecting what you have when you can barely make ends meet. It will be challenging to nourish your vision and purpose when you sit in an office every day concentrating on just getting the job done.

These strategies contain simple rules and principles that you can use to produce immediate results. Following the sequence of the 21 action strategies can result in strengthening, protecting, accelerating, and nourishing your wealth and legacy for generations.

One idea I always have found useful when reading a book is to take time to write down ideas flowing into my head, time to think and reflect. As such, at various points in this book, there are action steps that will allow you space and time to immediately capture your thoughts or emotions about the ideas being presented.

The Magic of Money: 21 Simple Actions to Make Money and Keep Money is a journey of a thousand steps. Sit back, relax, and let's take that first step together.

ACTION STRATEGY 1
MASTER FINE DISTINCTIONS

"Man who catch fly with chopsticks can accomplish anything."
—Pat Morita in *The Karate Kid*

Mastery. It sounds daunting, out of reach, beyond our grasp. Like much of what we do in life, attaining mastery begins with a first step. What is mastery? How do we achieve it? How do we know when we have it? A fine wine, a baseball player swinging effortlessly at a 95 mile per hour fastball for a home run, a 140 mile an hour tennis ball served at an opponent for an ace. The professionals make it look effortless, easy. What is unseen and unknown by most people are the countless thousands and thousands of hours spent preparing and training. What is hidden is the sacrifice of time and of other pleasures, the injuries and the heartbreaks, in order to be the best, to be different, to stand out and to stand in mastery. Michael Phelps, winner of 18 Olympic gold medals, once said, "While you were going to school, I was swimming. While you were going out on dates, I was swimming. While you were going to parties, I was swimming." Michael Phelps' dedication to his sport led him to mastery. Dedication to your art, career, job, and family can make you a master as well.

Malcolm Gladwell in his book *Outliers: The Story of Success* discusses the idea that it takes 10,000 hours to master an activity. That's 8 hours every day, 40 hours every week, every week (except two) for a year, every year for 5 straight years. Every hour, every day, every week, every month, every year.

After completing my program in tax law, one of my first jobs was working for a midsize law firm. I was placed in the corporate department, forming corporations, drafting business agreements, and conducting tax analysis. I will never forget one of my first assignments, which was to file a form that exempted small businesses from having to register the stock with the Securities and Exchange Commission. To make sure I was filling out the form correctly, like any good attorney, I began my research of the law by delving into the appropriate code sections. The

14

irony is that the form required was one page long and took the experienced legal secretarial staff about one minute to complete. They knew how to fill out the form better than I did.

Welcome to my first step of mastery and the thousand-mile journey of practicing law. All the training of young, wide-eyed attorneys coming out of law school. We didn't know much of anything. I have now been in practice for over 30 years. When I say it, it's hard to believe. That's about six times over in mastery. Based on my educational background, my training, and the countless hours spent working with clients and bettering myself, I am proud to say that I stand within the top two to three percent of attorneys in the nation in the field of tax law. And even with all this training, I continue to learn and to grow and to be more valuable, and that is the best part.

How much time do you put into your activities? Where are you in your job, your career, your business, your sport of choice? How much time have you put in, and how much time do you put in to master all the little distinctions that are necessary for you to achieve mastery?

Some of the top professionals in music or sport have been quoted saying that if they fail to practice one day, they know the difference. If they fail to practice for two days, their critics and colleagues know the difference. And if they fail to practice for three days, the public knows the difference. The distinctions are that small when you have achieved that level of mastery. You may already be wondering how it is possible to achieve this level of mastery. So much time has gone by. We aren't getting any younger.

ACTION STEP

To overcome any doubt about your ability to achieve mastery, let's do an exercise and look at how many incredible positive results you have accomplished in your life, your family, your job, or your business. This exercise will help show how capable you are. It's a confidence booster. Take a few moments and write down some of your highest and greatest accomplishments, ones that give you the most pride and pleasure. List some of the hard work you had to put in. Note some of the people who were around you when you were making the accomplishments. What did you have to sacrifice and what have been the rewards?

_____

_____

_____

_____

_____

_____

_____

_____

_____

_____

_____

_____

_____

_____

I have been a snow skier my entire life. Our ski trips were always at resorts—in California, Colorado, even Europe—where the runs were groomed and the places to ski were fixed according to the rules of the resort. I never had the experience of skiing off-piste, away from the regular ski runs, until I had the opportunity to go helicopter skiing in Canada. It was the chance of a lifetime and a trip I will never forget. No chairlift lines. No groomed runs. Powder skiing through trees, led by a guide. Danger of avalanche, yes, but risks were assessed and managed. On this trip of 40 people, I was probably one of the least talented, and I considered myself an expert skier. We had ski instructors, former ski racers, ski patrollers, kids from Switzerland doing flips off cornices. The first couple of days, let's just say I was a little out of my comfort zone, learning the avalanche beacon, trudging through powder, and getting buffeted by the wind of the helicopter as it set down to pick us up. However, as with all things in life, step by step I gained confidence, my ski rhythm improved, and by the third day I was enjoying this incredible journey. I look back on this trip and other events and realize what can be accomplished, and I use this as a marker to propel myself forward to the goals I want to accomplish in the future.

Mastery. What is mastery? Defining mastery is useful so that we all have a common point of reference. Mastery has six distinctions:

Commitment

Excellence

Intensity, Repetition, Frequency

Innovation

Mastery Distinction Number 1: COMMITMENT

Commitment is a mindset. It's doing something long after the newness has worn off. It's doing something even when the going gets tough. For example, imagine you are a C level tennis player and you want to reach B level. Commitment means taking lessons and playing the better players. With a 100 percent commitment, if you fail to reach the B level right away, you will know that it wasn't due to a lack of commitment, but rather a lack of knowledge, skill, or training. Without a 100 percent commitment, however, if you fail to reach the B level right away, you won't really know whether it was due to a lack of commitment or a lack of knowledge, skill, or training. What is your level of commitment to what you are doing or what you want to do in your life? I once read a phrase that I thought was very appropriate to this idea of commitment: you only commit once to doing something. Anything else is not a commitment.

Mastery Distinction Number 2: EXCELLENCE

Excellence is aiming to be the very best. It doesn't mean that you have to be the very best, but if you want to attain mastery in any field, the willingness, ability, and sacrifices required will be great. Although perfection would be ideal, it's also unattainable. Hence there is a saying: "Aim for perfection, settle for excellence." Reach for the stars and settle for the moon. In my field there are about 1.2 million attorneys in the U.S. About 75% of those are in private practice, which is about 900,000. Of those, 160,000 are in California. I had to estimate, given a lack of information, but let's assume that 20% do estate planning. The result is 180,000 in the country or 32,000 in California. Probably 10% of those have an advanced degree in tax law, as I do, which would be 3,200 in California (or 18,000 nationwide). That's 2% (3,200 of 160,000 in California, or 18,000 of 900,000 nationwide). With my advanced degree in taxation and 30 years of practice and experience, this puts me in the top 2% of attorneys in practice in the state and the country. I don't present this to boast. I mention it to show how much time and effort it takes to be excellent in your field. How are you aiming for perfection and what are you doing to be excellent in your life and business?

Mastery Distinction Number 3: INTENSITY

Intensity is like adding more weight, pushing your personal limits, beating your personal best. I can't imagine not wanting to get better. When I play tennis, I can't help myself. I have to coach others, and many times I get myself in trouble with those who don't want to be coached. If I see something that I think can help a person to hit a better ball or be in better position, I can't help myself; I have to say something. Many players don't approach the game this way. Their level of intensity is lower. They come on the court, they hit a few balls, they talk about politics or social problems, solve the world's ills, and they go home. Pushing themselves to get better is not as important, and there is nothing wrong with that belief. Nevertheless, these players won't reap the same benefits as those who are constantly pushing themselves, pushing their limits, pushing all of their muscles to the point where they are sweating, can barely walk, letting it all out on the court, pushing themselves to be the absolute best that they can possibly be. That is what intensity is about. Win or lose, it makes no difference; it's about how one goes about the process of becoming the best that he or she can be.

Mastery Distinction Number 4: REPETITION

Repetition can best be illustrated by people who work out at a gym. When they go to a gym and they lift weights, usually they will lift a certain number of pounds for a given number of times. That is repetition. For example, they will bench-press 150 pounds and do 20 lifts, and they may do three or four sets of these repetitions. Professional tennis players hit thousands of balls at a time, sometimes working on just one stroke. Basketball players will shoot thousands of free throws, all from the same place, using the same motion. At first, doing repetitions may seem difficult, clunky, or awkward, but after doing the reps over and over and over again, technique becomes more natural, turning smoother and more effortless as muscle memory gets burned into the body. What repetitions are you doing in your life, job, career, or business that are propelling you forward to mastery?

Mastery Distinction Number 5: FREQUENCY

Following repetition is frequency. Frequency is how often you go to the gym or train in your skill. How many of you have ever gone to the gym, or the tennis court or the golf course, and worked out really, really hard, sweat dripping down your body, muscles fatigued and exhausted, and after that day you were fit for the rest of your life? Not too many, I imagine. That's because we all know that health, just like mastery, is a continuous maintenance process. (Nutrition works the same way.) It's something that gets built up or torn down over extended periods of time. As I get older, if I take a week off of tennis, it takes me two or three times of play to get back some of the little distinctions to which I have become accustomed. How well we build something up is based on the habits we create and the decisions we make on a day-to-day basis. What decisions are you making that are affecting your life, and are those decisions taking you on a path toward mastery?

Mastery Distinction Number 6: INNOVATION

Innovation is the true mark of mastery. I am fortunate in that I am a very strategic thinker. I see solutions, and I can't figure out why we have to go through all the fuss and battle to get to the result. When a client comes into the office with something that concerns them, I talk through the ideas and then we make a plan to arrive at a solution. Innovation is coming up with brand-new ideas for already existing marketplaces or creating new ideas for brand-new marketplaces. Ideas that allow you to maximize results or maximize efficiency.

When you master each strategy in *The Magic of Money*, it will be like muscle memory. You won't have to think about it. You will have the proverbial unconscious competence. You will be at a point where you won't know how you are doing something so well. It will be effortless and easy.

ACTION STEP

Take a moment and reflect on what you are doing in your life and business, and what you could be doing to attain mastery. Write down your thoughts. Let them flow. Don't judge, don't filter. Let your mind be free to allow the creativity that is in you to come out.

_____

_____

_____

_____

_____

_____

_____

_____

_____

_____

ACTION STRATEGY 2

MASTER EGO AND FIND YOUR TRUE SELF

Sigmund Freud, the famous psychoanalyst, developed new theories about human behavior and the inner workings of people's minds. He is famous for such principles as the Oedipus complex and the idea that we have three aspects to our personality: the id, the ego, and the superego. Each of these siblings, as I call them, has a purpose and wants to express itself. The first sibling is the id, which Freud defines as our passions or impulses. Each one of us has passions. Each one of us has impulses on which we want to act. Sometimes they may be hidden, but they are there. For anyone who doubts this, just think of one time when you were laughing heartily, enjoying a sport, reading, or doing something that was so pleasing you couldn't get enough of it. That's passion, and even if the other 99 percent of the time it may not show, it is there.

The second sibling is the superego or conscience. All the things we shouldn't do, should do, conformity, compliance with social norms and behavior. The purpose of the superego is to make sure the id doesn't get out of hand—and the id likes to get out of hand. Think spring break for college students.

Then there is the self-regulating mechanism. The middle child caught between the competing forces of the other two siblings. This is the ego. The ego has been characterized as the part of us that is realistic. Its purpose is to organize our thoughts and make sense of our surroundings, and in psychoanalytic terms, the ego will do whatever is necessary to make our surroundings make sense.

How these three siblings manifest themselves is quite novel. In the mind, there is a constant conflict between the three siblings. Sometimes this conflict produces anxieties, guilt, and disorders. Sometimes it shows up in making mistakes at critical points, nervousness in taking a test, choking on closing out a tennis match, failing to hit a one-foot putt in golf. The ego wants to avoid pain and conflict. It needs to make sense of the world. The ego will do everything it can to protect us. The problem is that in its zeal to protect us, the ego will deceive us. It will make up stories, give us rationalizations, reasons, and excuses not to do something that is perfectly desirable, like winning a sports match, competing in a speech contest, or performing well on an exam.

Fear of public speaking is an example of the ego's story. About 10 percent of people have a real phobia of speaking in public. Another 10 percent of people would do anything to get up on stage. That leaves the other 80 percent of us, and as the saying goes, we would rather be in the casket than delivering the eulogy. Some research suggests that it goes back to our biology. We are out in the open, unprotected, and the fight-or-flight syndrome kicks in. Our heart rate increases and our breathing gets faster. Twenty million years of evolution and we still can't tell the difference between a saber-toothed tiger and a speech. Will you be judged, scorned, laughed at, ridiculed? To protect the fragile human host, the ego says you are afraid of standing up in front of a group, and you accept that as true. Where did this story come from? Who said it? Why is it true?

I was at a seminar where the speaker asked the audience who was terrified of public speaking. A woman raised her hand. The speaker asked her to stand up and give us her name and what she did for a living. He asked a few more questions. She was talking easily about herself. The speaker pointed out that she had just stood up and talked in front of a large audience. Then he had her come on stage and do the same thing again. So much for the fear of public speaking.

What stops most people from taking action is the ego voice inside of them. The ego voice is the human defense shield. The ego wants to protect us from all the bad things that people might think or say about us. It's that little voice that says we are too good to be doing that kind of work. We are going to wait for our big chance. It's too hard; it takes too much time. I would rather sit and watch television, go broke, have nothing, and blame it all on someone else. That's easy. That's ego.

How does the ego know when to act up? The answer comes from what we are taught and learn as we grow up. For example, in the classroom the conditioning to a question is to give a correct answer. What happens when the correct answer is not provided? Students laugh, the teacher tells us we are wrong, and then moves on. From this experience comes the learned behavior not to raise our hand because we will look foolish and be ridiculed. It's no wonder that when a person stands in front of a room, all those feelings rise to the surface. Stories and experiences like this become the ego's supply house of material in which to keep a person from speaking in public. Are you better at speaking one on one with a person? If so, why? And if you can speak to one person, why not 50 or 100 or 1,000?

What if we could make the ego go away, as in e ... go? Get out of here. Stop giving false stories. Stop telling us that something can't be done when we know full well that it can. How much difference would it make in our life if we recognized when the ego was acting against our best interests, and with full conscious awareness we could put the ego away? Some of you may be wondering how this can be done. You already have the answer. Go back to the exercise where you listed all the wonderful positive accomplishments in your life. You did these. Some easily, some with hard work, but all without the little voice saying, "This is one I can't do."

When my wife and I were attending our son's freshman orientation, we were in a room of about 1,000 parents. The speakers were getting ready to do a skit and they asked for a volunteer from the audience. From the back, I surveyed the room, looking left, looking right. As you can imagine, not one hand went up ... except mine. Just three months earlier, I had joined an organization to train my speaking and seminar skills. I use the word training intentionally here, because my ultimate goal was to become a professional in this industry. I wanted to find a message that meant something and deliver that message. In just three months of training, coming up on stage was like a drug. I was given lessons and skills and multiple opportunities to be on stage with a microphone in front of people. I couldn't get enough. My hand went up, and I participated in a skit in front of 1,000 parents.

The work I do now is a reflection of over five years of training with Frontier Trainings. I use exercises and games to get across lessons, because when people are active and engaged in learning, just like when we were kids playing games, the lessons are remembered longer. I have learned powerful techniques in using our body to amplify our speaking message, and I have learned how to create a virtual reality out of the speaking area where I am giving speeches.

When it comes to money, the ego can do real damage. If you were taught that money doesn't make people happy and you want to be happy, then you can't have any money? Really? So all the millionaires out there are unhappy. As you read this, you are probably starting to laugh a bit and think how ridiculous it is.

The most valuable work is to figure out how to make the e ... go. What teachings and experiences did you have as a child growing up? What conflicts are they creating and how can you smooth them over so the ego won't have to stand in the way? For me, winning a tennis match created some real conflict. Some deep-seated fear of success, I guess. This fear popped up in singles, where it was one to one, *mano a mano*. It wasn't until I was in my late 40s and into my 50s that I was able to reconcile my conflicts, recognize my ego talking, make the e ... go, and move on to win matches. In the pages that follow, I will be exploring various principles of behavior and thinking, how they get in the way, and what we can do to overcome them.

ACTION STRATEGY 3

IT'S ALL IN YOUR MIND

In what seems like the blink of an eye, the choices we make in the past always catch up to us in the future. Maybe we work late at the office instead of going to our son's baseball game or our daughter's dance recital. We make promises to take a vacation or go out for a family dinner, and at the end of the month we feel the pain of not being able to keep those promises. We get divorced, file for bankruptcy, and in the end we wonder what we have left and what we have accomplished.

Does it seem like we are struggling harder and harder to make ends meet? That vacation in Paris has turned into a staycation at home, sitting on the couch having a French experience; drinking French wine, eating french fries, and watching Pepé le Pew find romance.

Are you overwhelmed in running your business? Do you wear so many hats that it feels like you have a multiple personality disorder? Are you on time management overload? When we lack a clear direction, it can feel like we are chickens running around with our heads cut off.

We have high hopes for our business and our life. Freedom to be our own boss. Freedom to provide value the way we want, and freedom to make a better life. Unfortunately, competition, taxes, and regulations are strangling those hopes and turning dreams into just ... dreams.

What choices are you making and what will be your legacy? In the end, everyone leaves a legacy. The only question is whether it will be one of your own choosing and one that will make you proud. Isn't that why we are here? Isn't that why we work so hard? We work hard not so our wealth and legacy can be blown away like the sands of time. No, we work hard so our wealth and legacy can last not just one generation, not just two generations, but three generations and beyond.

Just as it sounds, *The Magic of Money* is a strategy to take care of what's upstairs in our mind, because when we take care of what's in our mind, we can take care of what's in our wallet.

After a long career in tax law, owning a money management company and getting involved in transformational work, using exercises and games to get across lessons so they will be remembered longer, I recently began doing reading and research in behavioral economics. This body of work drills down into how our behavior influences our money. From my learning, I created four behavioral types to reflect some of the barriers that stand in the way of building wealth and nourishing legacy.

Behavioral type one: The Intellectual

The Intellectual talks using complex principles and terms that are hard to understand. Collateralized mortgage obligations or derivatives, investment diversification, standard deviations in stock trading. Good grief, I just want something simple. When the Intellectual shows up, making matters too complex, people have a tendency to avoid them. Estate planning, tax planning, financial planning, organ donation. It's not that people don't know it's important; it's just that there are too many decisions, and they shut down. I don't know too many people who go to a cocktail party and say, "You should see the estate plan I just completed—48 pages of black print on white paper, with a blue signature and a colored binder. Now we are talking." But what if you could go to a cocktail party and, while others are lamenting that they have no plan, that their kids don't understand how to manage their finances, you could confidently say that not only do you have a plan and a strategy, but that your family is prepared for wealth?

The way to overcome the Intellectual is through the KISSAR principle. Keep it simple, stupid, and relevant. Think of something you like to do. How much do you do of the thing you like to do? My guess is a lot. You read, you engage, you do all you can to get more of the thing you like to do. When something is relevant to someone, they will do a lot of it. Keep it simple: buy low, sell high; avoid taxes; protect your legal backside; improve yourself, improve the world. Cash is king.

If you find estate planning, financial planning, and tax planning too overwhelming, Legacy Legal can keep it simple and relevant, taking very complex ideas and finding strategies and ideas that will simply work for you.

Behavioral type two: The Couch Potato

The Couch Potato has a common lament: "I don't want to. I will do it later. Don't bother me." There are some real negative consequences of being a Couch Potato when it comes to building wealth. The table below shows the difference between an early and a late start in investing.

AGE	YEARLY	INVESTED	TOTAL RETURN
5–6	$2,500	$5,000	$1,598,000 at 10%
5–18	$2,500	$35,000	$6,785,000 at 7%
25–35	$5,000	$50,000	$540,000 at 7%
35–65	$5,000	$150,000	$602,000 at 7%
25–65	$5,000	$200,000	$1,142,000 at 7%

The way to overcome the Couch Potato is … wait for it … get off the couch. Just get started. A body in motion tends to stay in motion. Research in behavioral economics suggests that to help overcome the procrastination syndrome requires that deadlines be imposed on us to get us into action. I would also offer that if we can show someone that a pain is too great or a benefit is too valuable, they will also be moved to action. What is the cost to you of staying on the couch watching television for hours at night instead of reading a book or playing or talking with the children? How much life or money do you lose? How much do you sacrifice by not taking action? What is your goal or dream in life? I am quite sure it is not to lie on your deathbed and say you stayed on the couch all your life. If you want something, you are going to have to get off the couch and do it.

To help get you into action, here are some simple tips. First, pick a date and time that you will complete a chosen action. Second, work backward and determine each step that will be required in order to complete the action. Third, for each step determined, set a date and time for taking that step. To keep yourself motivated, pick a reward for each time you achieve the date and time objectives. Also, pick a penalty for each time you *don't* achieve a date and time objective.

Behavioral type three: The Crybaby

"I want it now, I want it now." Nice house, nice car, nice clothes. Immediate gratification. We have become a consumer-oriented society, laden with debt. In business, here is how the Crybaby shows up. Picture a hamster on a wheel. Make more money, make more money, make more money. The problem is, there's a hole in the bucket; spend more money, spend more money, spend more money. In one end and out the other. There is a principle based on Parkinson's Law which says that people will tend to spend to the limit of their income. To build wealth, there has to be money left over with which to build wealth, which means that it is imperative to fight Parkinson's Law. If you take a penny and double it for 30 days straight, the value of that penny becomes $5,368,709.12. Why is it then that some business owners struggle for 30 or 40 years and sometimes never hit that first million?

To overcome the Crybaby, we need to provide security. Security in knowing that everything will be all right.

People will usually favor present rewards and benefits over future ones when they don't or can't see the greater value of the future reward. However, if you were certain you could build wealth, would you take the steps today to achieve it right now? If you were certain that you could protect your wealth and possessions, would you take the steps to achieve it right now? If you were certain that you could nourish a legacy, would you take steps to achieve it right now?

Are you ready to build wealth? Are you ready to protect your home, your investments, your business? Are you ready to nourish a legacy?

The Magic of Money can support you in building wealth. *The Magic of Money* can support you in protecting what you own. *The Magic of Money* can support you in nourishing your legacy.

It's not what you make but what you keep that counts. When you are walking down the street and you see a penny on the ground, do you pick it up? If not, why not? Is it not enough? Are you too good? The irony of the penny is that it's free. You don't have to work for it, other than bending down. You don't have client acquisition costs. You don't have to network. It's free, and you are that much richer for it. How many pennies are you leaving on the ground in your life and your business?

One day, I was in line at Panera getting ready to order my breakfast when I saw a dime and a penny on the ground. My first reaction was, "What will people think if I pick it up?" That lasted about two seconds, as I realized I didn't care what people thought. I bent down and I was eleven cents richer for doing nothing. How much richer can you be by building wealth so that later on you don't have to do anything? Cash is king. The idea of building wealth is to have sufficient assets paying you a monthly amount that takes care of your needs in accordance with your lifestyle. Think about that. You get to do whatever you want because your monthly income needs are met. That's what building wealth is all about. That's why overcoming the Intellectual, the Couch Potato, the Crybaby, and as we will see, the Miser, is so important.

The security needed to overcome the Crybaby requires five keys.

Key number one: Income and Expense Compass. I have included in Appendix 1 at the end of this book an income and expense compass that we use for business owners.. You have to know how much money you make and how much money you spend. Once you know this, you will know if you are actually keeping any money, because it's not what you make, it's what you … keep. In greater depth you can look at where you can save even more money.

Key number two: Commitment. Remember the commitment in mastery. Once you commit, you commit. No going back. Commit to what you will do, whatever that is.

Key number three: Pay yourself first. The only way to build wealth is to build wealth. If you don't pay yourself first, chances are you won't have any money left to pay yourself, and if you have no money to pay yourself, then you cannot possibly build wealth.

Key number four: Make it automatic. Set up an automatic payment from your bank account into the buckets I will describe below.

Key number five: The bucket list. What do you do with the money you now know you can save? Many financial advisors talk about buckets, and I will as well.

Bucket number one: The fun bucket. This first bucket may surprise you. The reason we have a fun bucket is because we all need to satisfy at least some of our desires for immediate gratification. The fun bucket gives us certainty that we will have some pleasure and not sacrifice everything we like. Who would want to do that? When I started this process and put aside money in a fun bucket, at the end of the month my wife and I went to a Chinese restaurant. As we moved through dinner and a glass of wine, I realized I couldn't spend enough of my fun bucket. I ordered a second glass of wine. I felt liberated, knowing that I could truly enjoy myself and still have money left over.

Bucket number two: The saving bucket. This is a bucket in which we save for a short-term goal like a vacation or new furniture. Very simply, I have a savings account and I am putting money away for a one-week ski vacation with my son in Telluride, Colorado.

Bucket number three: The investment bucket. This is the bucket that you don't touch. As your investments grow, eventually the goal will be for those investments to generate the income you need or want to meet your future lifestyle needs.

Bucket number four: The dream bucket. The dream bucket is that special thing you have always wanted.

Let's review. With the income and expense compass you will know how much money you have left over after you take care of your living expenses. You will now commit to moving the extra money over to four buckets, and you will do this through an automatic bank account transfer.

Most likely, the question you are asking at this point is "How much should I put into each bucket?" Here is the rule of thumb. For the investment account, you should put ten percent of the money that comes in. If you are on a regular salary, then it's ten percent of each paycheck. If you are in business, then it's ten percent of the sales. Then you put a similar percentage into your spending, your saving, and your dream bucket, so that you are living off of sixty percent of what you make. Of course, if this is not possible, then adjust the percentages to what is comfortable for you without completely sacrificing having a little fun. The key, though, is to develop the habit of making sure you put some amount away every time into your investment bucket, because this is the one that will help you build wealth.

Behavioral type four: The Miser

"It's mine, it's mine." Once we own something valuable, we tend to place a greater value on it than others might, and we don't want to give it up. It can be very painful every time we do. However, there is an irony about money. If money sits under the mattress, it is not in action. Money only has value if it is in action. Under the mattress it is dead money and isn't doing you any good. Technically, equity in your home is what is called dead equity. It doesn't do you any good. As we saw in the Great Recession, people who couldn't pay their mortgage, even if they had equity in their home, still lost the home. People who had paid their mortgage religiously for years, but then ran into some hard times, lost their homes because the banks weren't in the business of giving you a break. When you have fully paid for your home, then no one can take it away from you. There are many strategies to save you lots of money in repaying your mortgage, but they are beyond the scope of this book. Keeping money in a savings or investment account is keeping it in action, because it is earning interest or dividends or growth, and the bank or company in which the money was invested is using it for other purposes.

To overcome the Miser requires certainty. The Miser needs to know that the money will be protected. There are many ways to protect money. I will present three strategies here.

Strategy number one: Prepare an estate plan. An estate plan provides comfort in knowing how your family will be prepared for wealth should you become disabled or when you leave this planet. An estate plan provides certainty in the knowledge of how your hard-earned wealth will be distributed to family or others, and the way it should be distributed. (Note: With 30 years of tax and estate planning experience behind me, my personal opinion and belief is that organizations promoting self-prepared estate planning do a disservice to people and could lead to greater troubles and money problems down the road. My training and experience gives me a unique ability to navigate the minefields that can blow up your plans when you don't understand the terminology and the implications of what you are doing.)

Strategy number two: Protect your legal backside. If you run a business, most likely you should set up some type of entity structure, such as a corporation or limited liability company. Again, the nuances and distinctions should be discussed with a qualified professional. I would also be careful which professional you use. While certified public accountants are very knowledgeable, they are not lawyers and may not understand all the legal rules regarding which entity is better. In addition, not all lawyers understand the full tax law implications in the different kinds of entities. Making sure you get the right advice is essential. I am trained not only in law but also in tax law, which gives me a significant advantage in that I can bring a greater wealth of knowledge and value to your particular situation.

Strategy number three: Communicate. Communicate your plans to your family. That doesn't necessarily mean you tell them everything about what you own and your money, but certainly you can talk about your plans in general. Communicate with them about wealth building. Get them to understand that the benefits of putting money away now will make them millionaires later on. Throughout my career I have seen countless times when people put their plans in place, then placed them on the shelf, only to find them partially or totally useless when the time came to use them, because there was a failure to communicate the plans within the family.

I would like to share a success story of the G family. In this family, Grandma and Grandpa had accumulated sizable real estate holdings. Grandpa died with a basic estate plan. After the family came to me for a review of the plan, it was apparent that on Grandma's death, the family might incur a significant estate tax. Therefore we created a plan to avoid this result. Over the years, everything went well with the plan. As Grandma got older, I suggested that a family meeting be held to discuss the ideas of legacy and the meaning of the plan. Grandma hesitated at first. The family had become comfortable with me as a tax attorney, but the idea of doing family legacy planning was as they said: They liked the old Rich. As Grandma reached her nineties, she realized that having a family gathering might be valuable, particularly in light of the fact that the granddaughter was the one running the family real estate business, which meant that she would be smack-dab in the middle of having to deal with all the various family member needs and desires. The meeting took place. It went very smoothly, with all family members understanding what the plan meant and agreeing as to how it would positively affect them.

- Keep it simple, stupid, and relevant to overcome the barrier of an Intellectual;
- Get started to overcome the barrier of a Couch Potato;
- Create security for the Crybaby; and
- Provide certainty for the Miser.

With these steps, your ability to overcome barriers, build wealth, and nourish legacy is inevitable.

ACTION STRATEGY 4

MIND CLOGS

As if our ego and behavioral barriers weren't enough, there are other parts of our personality that can clog our mind and keep us from overcoming barriers in our life, building wealth, and nourishing legacy. I describe these clogs as RUST, where R stands for root clogs, U stands for upbringing clogs, S stands for story clogs, and T stands for trait clogs.

RUST

These clogs are deep-seated parts of our psychology that keep us from doing what we want to do. In this section, there are some very important exercises which require that you be in a quiet place with time to ponder. During this time it will be helpful to have at hand a journal or paper. When doing the exercises, don't worry about whether what you write is good or bad, right or wrong. There are no judgments. No one is looking. It's just you and your self. The best thing you can do is simply to write down what comes to your mind. Get it out in the open.

Root Clogs—The Unconscious

Root clogs are the unconscious part of our brain in which we do things without realizing why we are doing them. In some ways, the unconscious reveals itself through our dreams, and there is a whole body of psychoanalysis and psychology devoted to understanding the true meaning of our dreams. Some of the behaviors that manifest themselves out of the unconscious include our need for acceptance, arrogance, envy, being judgmental, narcissism, and how we perceive ourselves.

Upbringing Clogs—The Money Personalities

Upbringing clogs are behaviors that come from our culture, where we grew up, the parents and friends we had, the beliefs and values we took in. The upbringing clogs have a significant impact on how we view money and build wealth. There are four upbringing clogs.

Upbringing clog one: The Pirate

Pirates are carefree. They do what they want when they want. They love to spend money, pillage, and live life large. They play full out. Spending money is not a concern to them. Pirates love to party, entertain, and have fun. Those things cost money. Are you a Pirate? Do you pick up the bill for your friends at restaurants? Do you buy the drinks? Would you rather go out to dinner than stay at home and cook? Understanding whether you are a pirate personality is a good way of understanding whether you are in a position to build wealth.

Upbringing clog two: The Caregiver

The Caregiver takes care of others. In the money sense, the Caregiver takes care of money by putting it in the bank, investing it, protecting it, but never spending it. The Caregiver saves. Caregivers want to make sure that emergencies are provided for, that there is enough money for food, education, and the essential needs in life. The Caregiver takes refuge in their home, safe and secure, and they fail to fully enjoy all the fruits of life. What is the benefit of protecting money when it comes at a cost of not having any (or limited) fun in life?

Upbringing clog three: The Channeler

The Channeler is the spirit of the universe. The Channeler wants all people to find their chosen path. The Channeler isn't really concerned with money. Have some, not have some, it doesn't matter as long as life's river of energy flows. Channelers feel money isn't needed. They reject it. If you have a Channeler personality, you may believe money is bad, it is evil, or it isn't important. One area where I see this is in the nonprofit world. Many nonprofit organizations and the people who work for them don't believe money is the answer. They believe that we need more love and support. While this is true—we do need more love and support—imagine how much more good you can do by having money than not having it. If you are a Channeler and your attitude is that you don't care whether you have money, guess what? You don't have any money.

If you are a Channeler personality, it might be helpful to look at the reasons why money is not important to you. Does it represent a contradiction of your beliefs? Do you think that having money will reduce the amount of spiritual love you can hold for others?

If that were true, then how does that explain all the benefits that the millionaires and billionaires create through their charitable foundations or charitable contributions and work?

Take the story of Ray Kroc. The Ray Kroc story is a great example of how money, success, and charity can go together. In 1917, 15-year-old Ray Kroc lied about his age in order to join the Red Cross as an ambulance driver in World War I, but the war ended before his training finished. He then worked as a piano player, a paper cup salesman, and a multi-mixer salesman. In 1954, he was presented with a whopping order for eight multi-mixers from a restaurant in San Bernardino, California. He went to see what this restaurant was all about, and he was introduced to a small but successful enterprise run by brothers Dick and Mac McDonald. Ray was stunned by the effectiveness of their operation. They produced a limited menu, concentrating on just a few items—burgers, fries, and beverages—which allowed them to focus on quality at every step.

Kroc pitched his vision of creating McDonald's restaurants all over the United States to the brothers. In 1955 he founded the McDonald's Corporation, and five years later bought the exclusive rights to the McDonald's name. By 1958, McDonald's had sold its 100 millionth hamburger.

Prior to his marriage to Joan Kroc, he established the Ray Kroc foundation to support research and treatment of alcoholism, diabetes, and other diseases. He established the Ronald McDonald House foundation. He was a major donor to the Dartmouth Medical School.

After his death, his entire fortune went to his wife, Joan B. Kroc. Continuing her former husband's legacy of giving, Joan Kroc established the Joan B. Kroc Foundation, which donated $18.5 million to the San Diego Hospice Corporation (now known as San Diego Hospice and The Institute for Palliative Medicine). The donation covered the cost of planning, land acquisition (6.5 acres [26,000 m^2]), construction, and interior furnishings of the center.

In 2002, a large Salvation Army community center known as the Kroc Center opened to the public. This center had been funded by Joan Kroc to the tune of about $87 million. Later, she bequeathed an additional $1.6 billion to open Salvation Army Kroc Centers across the nation. This was the largest one-time gift ever recorded. Several institutions in the San Diego area are named after her, including the think tank Joan B. Kroc Institute for Peace and Justice at the University of San Diego, the St. Vincent de Paul Joan Kroc Center for the Homeless in downtown San Diego, and the Kroc-Copley Animal Shelter in the Morena District.

There is nothing wrong with having money which allows people to do really good work in this world, or to have charities to benefit other people. Having money and being spiritual are two principles that can be held in the same space. In fact, having money most likely makes it easier to do good work in the world.

Upbringing clog four: The Jester

The Jester can't stand to deal with money issues. Bills come and they go into a drawer. The Jester has no budget, doesn't balance the bank account, and avoids the subject at all costs. The problem with Jesters is that they end up with their water or gas turned off or paying lots of penalties in late fees. Ignoring reality doesn't work too well. The Jester kids around, never being too serious. The Jester hides behind a carefree "everything is rosy" attitude. The Jester goes about his life never knowing whether he is coming or going, or going or coming, and how much money he has. If you are a Jester personality and your bills are strewn all over the place, it's time to take control of those bills rather than letting them control you. I heard a great saying—that paying bills is a great thing, because it means you have money to have bills. Most people look at paying bills as a bad thing. "Sending money to other people, my bank balance is going down. Isn't that the whole point of living life and doing things you want to do?"

ACTION STEP

What areas of your upbringing are creating clogs for you?
Are you a Pirate or a Caregiver? A Channeler or a Jester?
What does money represent to you? What is your upbringing
personality? Take some time and think about your money
upbringing personality. How is it serving or not serving you?
What changes are necessary to make money work for you and
for you to obtain the value you richly deserve?

_____

_____

_____

_____

_____

_____

_____

_____

Story Clogs

Story clogs are the stories that you tell yourself, the excuses and reasons for why you behave the way you do. Avoiding pain, avoiding responsibility, feeling important, being right, getting sympathy, control, safe, easy, comfortable, acting busy, pity, and pride are all descriptions attributable to people who suffer from the story clogs. "Ohhhh, it's too hard. It wasn't my fault; I am right. You won't believe what happened to me today … my car broke down, I tore my clothes (sympathy factor). Do it my way or I don't want to go out; I like staying home," and so forth. A couple of examples of story clog personalities are the whiner and the drama queen. The whiner complains about every little thing, whether it's good or bad. The drama queen thrives on drama, of course. If something isn't being made out to look like the most important thing on earth, the drama queen just isn't happy. The key to understanding the story clogs is to think about what benefit you receive by telling the story. Is it protecting you in some way? Is it ego? What is the reason you tell the story? Because unless there is a reason, you wouldn't need to tell the story.

ACTION STEP

Take a few moments and write down the stories you tell yourself when you don't want to do something. Let's be candid. What excuses do you make and how does that affect your opportunities? How do they detract from what you can accomplish?

_____

_____

_____

_____

_____

_____

Trait Clogs

The trait clogs are the fourth type of clog in RUST. The trait clogs are the personality traits we exhibit, most of which we are clearly aware of, but which we act on and act out anyway.

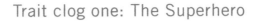

Trait clog one: The Superhero

"I am not going to die. I will do it later." Superheroes don't plan because they think they are invincible. When we act like a Superhero and fail to make a plan, then when we are no longer able to make a plan, either due to lack of mental competency or death, a plan will be made for us. That plan is usually made by people we may not want making the plan, and it's also a plan we probably wouldn't want. Some of the costs of acting like a Superhero include: FAIL = family anger in lawsuits, families ripped apart, brothers and sisters stop talking; FAIL = financial abundance is lost, and money that could be invested in the family is wasted on frivolous lawsuits; FAILURE = family achievement is lost, undermining real enrichment. People plan a vacation, they plan to buy a home, they plan to have a child, but when it comes to planning their wealth and legacy, they would rather listen to fingernails screeching on a chalkboard. A plan is like a map, providing a destination, the roads to take, and the hazards to watch out for.

Trait clog two: Wile E. Coyote

The second personality in the trait clogs is Wile E. Coyote. We all know Wile E. Coyote. A clever fellow, but it just seems that everything Wile E. did, didn't seem to work out. Here's the brain, here's the book, here's the scalpel, now go do the brain surgery. None of us would think of doing our own brain surgery, yet how many of us think we can take care of building wealth and legacy without the right professional training?

My Wile E. Coyote story involved landscaping. I set out to prepare a nice four-by-four-foot area to plant some plants where a tree once stood. I took axe and shovel in hand. Four hours later, I am still hacking away at tree roots. Of course, as I am hacking away, you know what happens next. I break the sprinkler pipe. Sometimes doing things yourself isn't the best course for building wealth and nourishing legacy.

Almost every time our law firm has worked with a client who attempted to prepare paperwork themselves or thought they understood terms that have very specific meanings in the context of legal and tax work, the client inevitably caused more problems than they solved. Then we had to do twice as much work to fix the problem. In one case in particular, I was working with a client who wanted to transfer a piece of real estate to a company he owned. During this time he got married and decided to transfer the real estate to his wife. What he didn't realize is that by doing so, he risked increasing the property taxes he was paying. It took time, money, and effort to undo the mistake.

Trait clog three: The Ostrich

The Ostrich goes about its business, makes plans, and then sticks its head in the sand, hoping everything will work out. A plan with no communication causes families to be ripped apart, brothers and sisters to stop talking, and money that could be invested in the family to be wasted on frivolous lawsuits.

Unfortunately, the cost of lack of communication played out in court for one family. The family had divorced parents, two brothers, and a sister. Communication in this family around money was poor. One of the brothers passed away. The other brother became the court-appointed representative, known as the administrator, to take care of the deceased brother's monetary affairs. The administrator suffered a severe accident. Sadly, because the communication in the family was poor, the administrator took, for his own personal use, all of the money from the deceased brother's estate, leaving the rest of the family with nothing.

In another unfortunate situation, a father made changes to his legal documents, giving his daughter an equal share of what he owned when he passed away. Unfortunately, he failed to communicate his wishes and changes to his other child. After the father's death, the changes were challenged by the son. The lawsuit dragged on for several years, with the brother raising all kinds of challenges and obstacles. He did this even after the parties entered into a supposed settlement. Lots of attorney fees and animosity was the legacy of this family and their failure to discuss the plan.

ACTION
STEP

Write down any trait clogs you have. Do you put off until tomorrow valuable planning? Do you plan and then go back to the same old habits? Do you like doing things yourself, without the benefit of the expertise of others? Write down the costs of doing so.

_____

_____

_____

_____

_____

_____

_____

_____

ACTION STEP

Next, what I want you do to is to take all of the individual pieces of what you have written about the different aspects of RUST and put them into a descriptive story, as if you were writing from the perspective of a third person. Tell the story as if someone else were writing about you. For example, "Rich was well educated and his family was a family of professionals. Rich had opportunities, and yet Rich had a clog ..."

When you are writing your story, don't hold back. Be open and honest with what you write. This description will be highly valuable and will give you the ability to take the first step toward unclogging and releasing the obstacles that hold you back, that get in your way, and that keep you from building wealth and nourishing legacy.

_____

_____

_____

_____

_____

_____

_____

_____

_____

_____

_____

_____

ACTION STRATEGY 5

UNCLOG WITH CLOG BUSTERS

When our mind is clogged with RUST, how can we possibly take the right steps, and the right actions at the right time to create the right financial, tax, and wealth plans for ourselves and our family? In these situations, we need some clog busters to overcome some of the barriers in our mind! I have identified six clog busters that you can use anytime you feel your mind is clogged. These clog busters are tools you can use to eliminate the clogs, release the blocks, and keep moving forward toward overcoming barriers, building wealth, and nourishing legacy.

Clog buster number one:
The Philosopher of Thought

What a man thinketh, he can become. Thoughts are things, and things are actionable. Thoughts are the precursor to action. If we change our thoughts, we can change our actions. How many times have we done an activity to the point where it becomes natural, unconscious, embedded in our muscle memory? Then we let our mind get in the way, and we start to actively and to consciously think about the thing that came so natural. In that situation we begin to question what we are doing, how we are doing it, and the result we want, rather than just letting it happen naturally and easily. Mistakes get made, performance decreases, and we begin to have an internal dialogue about how bad we are and how we could have allowed a mistake to happen. To overcome this "beat ourselves up syndrome," Denis Waitley, who is renowned for his work on leadership, having trained top-gun pilots and astronauts, put forth a very simple but effective idea. What if we simply give ourselves a reminder to rely on what our mind and body know naturally and therefore not think too much?

Here is an example of how this simple principle can be applied. Under pressure, a tennis player's serve can go a bit haywire. When the body tenses up, nothing can go right. A player may shank the ball, hit it long or into the net, and the miles per hour can go down dramatically. After playing tennis for most of my life, I can't say how many good serves I have hit, and yet sometimes my mind gets in the way. Using Mr. Waitley's principle, when I feel a bit tight, I now just simply tell myself to hit a first serve. That's it. A positive assertion to hit a first serve, because my mind and body know how to hit a first serve and how to hit it well. This simple idea relaxes me, takes all the questions and doubts out of my mind, and most often when I do this, I hit a good first serve. My thoughts become my actions. Think about what to do correctly, and your mind and body will follow.

A second example I like to use is skiing through trees. One may wonder how skiers can go down a hill through a whole forest of trees and not hit any. The simple answer is that where the eyes go, the body follows. If the focus is on the tree, the body will go right for the tree. And yes, that would hurt, if not possibly kill you. What we do instead is focus on the white of the snow between the trees where we want to make our turns, and this allows us to glide down the hill right past the trees. We trust our muscle memory in how to ski as we focus on where we want to go. Driving is a third example of this concept. Where you look is where you tend to steer your car. Drivers don't look right at the lines on the street when driving. Rather, they look ahead to where they want to go. As you look ahead, muscle memory kicks in and the car goes where you want it to.

67

Clog buster number two:
The Burning Cauldron of Passion

A burning desire is the fire that wakes you up early in the morning and keeps you up late at night. A burning desire has definite purpose and is not a fleeting moment. Without a burning desire, you have burnout. You have excuses and reasons. With burning desire, every day is greeted as an adventure and an experience.

Clog buster number three:
The Olympian of Commitment

Make a plan and do what you said you would do. I wanted to start playing higher-level tennis. My skill level was about 4.5, but most of the guys I played against in the club had played in tournaments or played in the junior ranks as kids, maybe even nationally. They were at a 5.0 level, or maybe even a 5.5 level. How was I going to compete with them? I started taking lessons. We also had a weekly group of players of different skill levels. At first, I could only compete on the lower courts, but step by step as my strokes became better, as my accuracy improved, as I developed better strategy, I competed equally with the better players.

Clog buster number four:
The Fox of Confidence

This is a story of the circus elephant and the fox. The circus elephant is a noble, regal creature. Yet, how is it that this massive creature is able to perform the way it does? When the circus elephant is a baby, its trainer pounds a huge stake into the ground. The trainer takes one end of a rope and ties it to the stake. The other end of the rope is tied to the baby elephant's leg. The baby elephant tugs, but it cannot break free of the post. It pulls as hard as it can, but it cannot break free. It struggles with all of its might, but it cannot break free. At some point the baby elephant gives up. It goes into a state of what is called "learned helplessness." It has learned to be helpless, that it can't do anything to break free of the post. As the elephant gets older, with one kick it could pull the stake out of the ground, but the elephant won't kick. It has learned helplessness.

Unlike the elephant, the fox was raised to be free in the forest with confidence. He tests his actions to see what works and what doesn't. He talks to the elephant of his adventures down by the lake watching the beavers build their dam, up in the mountains with the billy goats, and out in the forest with mother bear watching her cubs.

There are people in life who have had their confidence ripped away. It might have been due to physical abuse or emotional abuse. It might have been due to high expectations that could never be met. Whatever the reason, we all have times when we lack confidence. In these situations, I find many people use outside events as a justification not to take action. This is a fear-based mentality, like the elephant. By contrast, there are people who just seem to plunge forward in action, and the results do not matter, like the fox. They recognize that their worth and value are not based on the result but on the doing. These are people who come from an abundance-based mentality.

How do we instill an abundance-based mentality? How do we instill a sense of confidence? One way is to get little wins. For example, if there is no revenue coming in to your business, start small and get one sale. Having a bad day in your sport of choice? Focus on one shot, one ball. To me, confidence is proof that the mind wants you to be successful, because each time you succeed, each time you get those little wins, your mind starts to think, "Oh, I can do that. That worked." The more you do it, the more successes you have, the more confidence you get to do more.

I want you to ponder who you are, the circumstances of your life, your upbringing, your culture. I want you to consider whether you use reasons and excuses to avoid doing things or you forge ahead. Do you base your value on what you do rather than the result? I want you to work through this section and, if nothing else, create an awareness and recognition that you can be like the fox. One little win at a time. One success at a time. Realize you can.

Clog buster number five:
The Drill Sergeant of Discipline

Do the same things over and over again, and don't allow distractions to move you off course. Do it even when you don't want to.

I was supposed to go to a chamber of commerce event. As the day approached, I started having a case of the "I don't want tos." The day came. I went and I made the decision that I would look to meet the most influential people in the room. I looked around and I saw a table with a prominent real estate broker whose name is well recognized in the community. I brought a few of my books with me and had them in an open box. The realtor asked whether I thought the book was good. I kind of laughed and said, "Well, I think so. I wrote it." He asked if he could have one. I said, "Of course." He then asked for my autograph, and I wrote about his respect and good deeds in the community. I was being nonchalant, but I noticed out of the corner of my eye that he was reading what I wrote. He then touched me, extended his arm, and said, "Thank you." I acknowledged his gratitude. After the event I found myself walking to my car and I ended up striking up a conversation with the fire chief of the City of Carlsbad. To make a long story short, he asked if he could have one of my books, as he saw the other gentleman had asked for one. The point of this story is that I was disciplined to go to the chamber event even when I didn't want to go, and it turned into a very enjoyable time, giving me exposure that may pay dividends at some future date.

Clog buster number six: Pepé Le Pew of Perseverance

No matter what stood in his way, Pepé Le Pew was bound and determined to find romance and love. For those unfamiliar, Pepé Le Pew was a skunk in the old Looney Tunes cartoons.

Pepé thought a black cat was another skunk and would pursue the cat (who of course wanted nothing to do with Pepé) to the ends of the earth. Nothing stood in Pepe's way. He kept going even when the going was tough. As an old saying goes, the bones in the desert are found three feet from the edge of the highway, which means that a person usually quits right before they are about to find success. If you have value to others, you are invaluable, and you have to keep going even when you may not think there is value at the start and others say no.

As another old saying goes, "Winners never quit." Quitters never become winners.

At this time you have an opportunity to think about past events and how your thinking affected the decisions you made. In this exercise, write down 20 significant events in your life. As you think about those events, consider what emotions and thinking you had that resulted in those events actually coming to pass. What was your decision-making process? As you write down the events, look for patterns and similarities in the events and your thinking. The purpose of this exercise is to make you aware of your thinking and how you might be making similar decisions today, resulting in actions you may not want. The purpose of this exercise is to show you how your thoughts can become actions. Passion and commitment coupled with drive and perseverance can break the clogs that keep you from your wealth and legacy.

To give you an example of how my thinking patterns sabotaged my success, back in 2000, in the heyday of the dot.com stocks, I was doing a lot of stock trading. In one case, I had a stock that had been recommended to me, and I kept buying as the stock kept going down. By the time it was at 50 cents, I went all in. I was either going to go broke or do very well. Within a few weeks the company announced a new CEO, and the stock rose to 3 dollars. I made $60,000 in one day. The sad part of this story, however, is that my patterns of thinking hadn't yet changed, and three months later the money was gone from my continued trading.

When I look back on the experiences that make up my life and some of my major turning points and decisions, I recognize how my clogs led to results that weren't necessarily the best ones. Similarly, I recognize how I changed the clogged patterns and results in my life and that I now have the opportunity to show others how to do the same. This is what I have to share in *The Magic of Money* and how these strategies do overcome barriers, build wealth, and nourish legacy.

ACTION STRATEGY 6

LIFESTYLE TREASURE MAP

Building wealth and nourishing legacy requires a good map. A map that will get you from one place to another. A good map will show you your destination. It will provide you with the roads to take, warn you of the hazards to watch out for, and show you the sights to see and enjoy. I realize there are some people who like to go on trips with no map. They will just go from place to place, enjoying being in the present. Sometimes that might be a great way to go, but not all the time. If you have no map, after a while, in my opinion, you will find yourself just wandering. A plan provides a framework; it provides structure. Within a plan there is flexibility and change, but you know that the ultimate destination can be assured as long as you stick to the plan.

In my Quick Start Guide, I provide a number of resources that you can use to prepare a good map. There is an income and expense compass, an asset temperature (see Appendix 1), a lifestyle plan and business plan templates that lead you step by step through the process of developing a sound map that will be your guide toward your goals.

ACTION STRATEGY 7

CLARITY IS LUCKY #7

Clarity keeps us focused. It helps us avoid hazards and it works in our favor in maintaining a clear direction. I have come up with seven clarities: purpose, vision, goals, action, leadership, legacy, and you. With the seven clarities, there is no doubting what you want and how you will get there. The seven clarities provide a strong framework to who we are and what we are willing to do.

Clarity number 1: The Clarity of Purpose

Purpose is the essence of who you are that makes you different from everyone else on the planet. What are your experiences, memories, and activities? What is it about you that makes you different from anyone else? Everyone on this planet is different. What in your background or how you were raised makes you different from everyone else? How can you use this difference to find a niche in the marketplace, a place for your products or services?

Clarity number 2: The Clarity of Vision

In my view, vision is a view of how to impact people and make a difference. All great leaders have a vision. Apple founder Steve Jobs had a vision to put a computer into the hands of everyday people. Through this vision he realized that people could have a different computing experience, a different way of interacting with a computer, and that is what led to Apple's different operating system. Bill Gates had a similar vision to have a computer in every home. More recently this vision has advanced to improving lives through technology.

Clarity number 3: The Clarity of Leadership

Leadership comes in many forms and many types. Jim Collins, a professor at the University of Boulder in Colorado and famous for his books, *Good to Great* and *Great by Choice,* found that there are 13 different types of leadership styles. I will list them here, and cover them in more detail in chapter 21.

Charismatic, Authentic, Mindful, Servant, Storytelling, Adaptive, Tribal, Level 5, Resonant, Emotionally Intelligent, Strengths-Based, No-Excuse, Narcissistic.

It is said that good leaders are able to rally people around a vision in line with a purpose. How are you a leader in bringing people together around a common purpose and vision?

Clarity number 4: The Clarity of Goals

Goals are like stepping stones. Each stepping stone you reach brings you closer to your goals in line with your vision and according to your purpose. Goals must be SMART: Specific, Measurable, Achievable, Results-Focused and Time-Bound. You can find out more detail about SMART goals in our Quick Start Guide available at www.mindmoneystrategy.com.

Clarity number 5: The Clarity of Action

What do you do each and every day to accomplish your goals? Remember the good old business plan (we will visit this in Chapter 8). That is a great place to start to look at what you need to do. Action steps are like making a peanut butter and jelly sandwich. In one training in which I participated, we were required to write out every key step in the process of making a peanut butter and jelly sandwich so that it could be understood by a Martian, so to speak. It took about 52 clean, clear steps. Write it out yourself if you don't believe me. Not only is it fun, but I guarantee you will learn something in the process. The Clarity of Action applies to your company and your systems. If a new person came into your company, would they know what to do if you weren't there? How to open the door, turn on the lights, start the coffee, get the conference room ready, and so forth? Step by step by step.

20-Mile March

Jim Collins, in his book *Great by Choice*, talks about a 20-mile march. It is based on a true story of two adventurers. One was Roald Amundsen, who marched 20 miles each and every day to reach the South Pole. Twenty miles no matter what the conditions. No more, no less. His team reached the South Pole and survived … in 1911. His competitor, Robert Falcon Scott, and his whole team, didn't fare as well. They marched longer on better days and shorter on others. They were ill-prepared with improper resources. All died. The lesson of this story is to get very clear on how you will attain your results each and every day, doing so with consistent, steady progress, regardless of economic conditions and obstacles. The 20-mile march is also a good benchmark for performance guidelines in a business. Did you achieve the benchmark, and if not, how do you make sure you can reach it the next time? What is your 20-mile march?

Clarity number 6: The Clarity of Legacy

How will you be remembered? What will you leave behind?

Clarity number 7: The Clarity of You

So often we hear about waiting until retirement to travel or do other activities we want to do. The challenge is that sometimes our bodies break down, our health deteriorates, or worse, and we never get to do those things or enjoy the opportunities in life. When I do seminars of one day or longer, being in shape and having energy is critical to my ability to be accessible to the students, run the exercises, and provide a great experience. How do you take care of yourself? What do you do just for yourself to treat and pamper yourself and renew your energy?

Here are my seven clarities.

Purpose

My purpose in life is to educate. Always has been. It's what I do best.

Vision

The vision in our company is to tap into the tremendous potential of business and family to build wealth and nourish legacy. Our mission is to change the way people think and talk about wealth, not only in money, but in values, beliefs, and traditions. We do this through our Membership Continuity Program, Quick Start Guide, seminars, books, and legal and tax services.

Leadership

In leadership I formed a partnership and began leading a boutique law firm. I chaired a group called the Business Legacy Mentoring Group. The purpose of the group was to bring business owners and entrepreneurs together in a networking setting where they would hear inspirational speakers, network, and get real-time business coaching all in one setting. I have been president of the local chapter of Business Networking International, a networking organization, and as of this writing I will be chairing the San Diego Speaker's Bureau Division of Toastmasters International.

Goals

My goals in business have been to build out interactive and fun seminars for business owners and entrepreneurs, and to build a community of like-minded people who like to learn and create more financial freedom in their life. I want to develop a team-based wealth management group to work with business owners and families at all stages to build wealth and nourish legacy with a view toward maintaining long-lasting relationships. For my personal life, I love to play tennis, ski, travel, and spend time with my family.

Action

The action steps to achieve my goals have included the following: Over the last seven years I have taken courses in business, speaking, sales, and personal transformation. I have read numerous books on living a more inspired life and leadership. I immersed myself in creating content, finding my message that I want to deliver to the world, and each day, month, and year focused my attention on these activities while maintaining a law practice which pays the bills.

Legacy

As for legacy (written from the third-person perspective): Rich would like to be known for living the embodiment of his life in integrity, values, and actions. Born to Jack and Lee Gaines, Rich was the third of three brothers. The family stressed education as a way to create a stable life. He went into tax law as a way to support people in keeping more of their hard-earned wealth.

After 25 years of doing work for people the "same old way," he was burnt out. He looked for a different way to find enjoyment. A different way to bring his knowledge, skills, and talent to people. After years of searching, Rich realized that family unity is a powerful force that can serve as a bedrock of unlimited possibilities. Each member of a family is unique, special, and families can make a difference. As Rich explored family, family dynamics, and how families can create a vision, a legacy, and be self-reliant, he founded Family Vision Adventures, where families and family businesses come together in an experiential learning environment where they receive skills, tools to overcome barriers, build wealth, create a vision, and a legacy.

Rich was a world-renowned speaker and trainer, traveling internationally and delivering his message of *The Magic of Money*. Rich established the Be Rich Foundation, which serves people in overcoming barriers, building wealth, and nourishing legacy.

Rich was married to Shelley. They had twins born on April 15. He leaves behind his wife and two children, four grandchildren, and eight great grandchildren. Rich's family is self-reliant and financially self-sufficient, with structures in place to assure that money, value, beliefs, and traditions will last for generations.

Rich was giving of himself—his time, his knowledge, and his experience—and always made time for others. He worked tirelessly until his death, but he always made time to pursue pleasures of travel, tennis, friends, and life's pleasures. He loved tennis, and attended all four Grand Slam tennis tournaments.

Rich was an inspiration to others, showing how one person can make a difference by influencing others through love. He is at peace with himself and his accomplishments. Through his journey, Rich found comfort in others and the knowledge that he stood out. He achieved all of his life's goals personally and professionally. Rich will be missed, but his legacy endures.

You

Rich took care of himself. He exercised and played tennis regularly, made sure he ate well, and used healthcare practitioners to keep his body in good shape.

ACTION STEP

Now it's your turn to write down your seven clarities.

_____

_____

_____

_____

_____

_____

_____

_____

_____

_____

_____

ACTION STRATEGY 8

DOUBT? WHAT DOUBT?
I HAVE A BUSINESS PLAN.

Rarely done, but so extremely valuable, is starting with the end in mind. When you are clear on what you want in the future, then you can work backward into the present and devise the plan of action to get you there. For example, if you are starting a business and you know you want to sell the business in the future for a certain amount of money, that clarity defines everything you will do to achieve that result. For the best result, in our Quick Start Guide is a comprehensive business plan. Take the sections of that workbook and insert them into the shortened framework here for you to have a concise business plan for your reference. The business plan has 13 parts, and each part has a list of items to help you be clear on what is being asked in each part.

Part 1: Executive Summary

Write down a summary of your business. What is the vision and mission of the company? A vision is a difference that you want to make. A mission is the defining purpose or way that you want to achieve the vision. For example, our company's vision is to tap into the tremendous potential of business and family to build wealth and nourish legacy. Our mission is to change the way people think and talk about wealth, not only in money, but in values, beliefs, and traditions. How long have you been engaged in your business? What are your primary products and services? What is the nature of the business today and what are its goals? What are the business's key success factors? What is the present legal and financial structure of the business? What is the present positioning of the company? Who are the owners, and what is the structure of management within the company? Since this is an executive summary and each of these areas is addressed in greater detail in the sections that follow, completing the more detailed sections and then coming back to this summary, taking a few sentences from each of the more developed sections, may be better.

_____

_____

_____

_____

_____

_____

_____

_____

_____

_____

_____

_____

_____

_____

Part 2: Department Summaries

For each department or division within your company, write down the vision and mission statements and the core values of that department.

_____

_____

_____

_____

_____

_____

_____

_____

_____

_____

_____

_____

_____

Part 3: Goals

What are the SMART goals for the business? Define SMART goals for each department or division within the company. SMART stands for Specific, Measurable, Achievable, Results-Focused and Time-Bound. Every goal has to be specific. A specific goal is defined by the what, why, and how. An example of a specific goal is "I want to ride my elliptical machine for 30 minutes every other day by August 1, 2015." The goal has to be measurable. One can measure whether I am riding the elliptical machine for 30 minutes every other day. Was it done or not? The goal has to be achievable. Clearly I can achieve this goal, meaning there is nothing inherently impossible with my achieving the goal. By comparison, I could never be an NBA basketball player. I don't have the physical abilities and height to do so. The goal must be results-focused. I know that by doing the 30 minutes of elliptical exercise every other day I will be in better health. Lastly, the goal must be time-bound. By a certain date. In this case, August 1, 2015. Very clear.

SMART Goal Questionnaire

Goal:

_____

_____

_____

_____

Specific. What will the goal accomplish? How and why will it be accomplished?

_____

_____

_____

_____

_____

_____

_____

_____

_____

_____

_____

_____

_____

_____

Measurable. How will you measure whether or not the goal has been reached (list at least two indicators)?

_____

_____

_____

_____

_____

_____

Achievable. Is it possible? Have others done it successfully? Do you have the necessary knowledge, skills, abilities, and resources to accomplish the goal? Will meeting the goal challenge you without defeating you?

_____

_____

_____

_____

_____

_____

Results-focused. What is the reason, purpose, or benefit of accomplishing the goal? What is the result (not activities leading up to the result) of the goal?

_____

_____

_____

_____

_____

Time-bound. What is the established completion date, and does that completion date create a practical sense of urgency?

_____

_____

_____

_____

_____

Revise your goal now that you've made it SMART:

_____

_____

_____

_____

_____

_____

_____

Part 4: Products/Services

List each product of the company. Provide a clear description of the product and how you position the product for sale. Evaluate the competitive positioning of the product. List each future product or service that you will have for sale.

_____

_____

_____

_____

_____

Part 5: Market Analysis

A market analysis will help you to determine the demographics (age, gender, income, etc.) and the psychographics (habits, likes, qualities) of your market for each product you sell or service you provide.

_____

_____

_____

_____

_____

_____

_____

_____

_____

_____

_____

_____

Part 6: Competitive Analysis

For each product or service, a competitive analysis will help you to determine if what you do is still a viable way to make money. Refer to the hedgehog principle, which is contained in my book *Business Strengtheners,* for more information on this principle. By addressing your competition and being prepared for change, you will be better able to meet it and succeed. Strengthening what you have requires knowing how you are going to compete and win.

_____

_____

_____

_____

_____

_____

_____

_____

_____

_____

Part 7: Strategy

What are your strengths and how do you intend to use those strengths? What are your weaknesses and how do you intend to bolster or support those weaknesses? For example, if you are not good at or don't want to do bookkeeping, then having a bookkeeper can be pretty important. What strategies are you using in your business to get better results?

_____

_____

_____

_____

_____

_____

_____

_____

_____

_____

_____

Part 8: Marketing and Sales

How will you market or sell your products and services? This will be your road map for ultimate implementation of the strategy.

_____

_____

_____

_____

_____

_____

_____

_____

_____

_____

_____

Part 9: Operations

Write down how your company operates. What roles do the people that work in the company have and what are their responsibilities? What facilities do you have and how do they operate? What is the organizational structure for the company?

_____

_____

_____

_____

_____

_____

_____

_____

_____

_____

_____

_____

Part 10: Financials

Figure out how much money is actually coming into the company and how much is going out.

_____

_____

_____

_____

_____

_____

_____

_____

_____

_____

_____

_____

_____

Part 11: Schedule

Each goal in your plan should have a time scheduled for when you want that goal to be finished and achieved.

Part 12: Action Plan

The action plan is the day-to-day activities that need to happen in order for you to hit the goals you have set out for yourself and step by step move you toward your vision and purpose. For each goal, write down each step that you think would need to happen in order for the goal to be achieved. For example, if the goal is to call ten more customers a week, then the action plan will define when the calls will be made, what will be said in those calls, how long the calls will last, how many calls will be made each day, and what kind of follow-up may be required. List as many actions as you think are necessary. It is better to have more than less. You can always delete certain actions as you check off the actions you accomplish.

_____

_____

_____

_____

_____

_____

_____

_____

Part 13: Accountability

Also vital is being accountable for your commitments and your actions. Do you hold yourself accountable or do you let yourself slide? What standard have you set for yourself? (Because what is acceptable becomes inevitable.) Some people suggest finding an accountability coach, partner, or friend. I am of the opinion that we are grown and mature adults, and we either hold ourselves accountable or we do not. You know whether or not you are doing something you are supposed to do, and the reasons or excuses you use are just a reflection of the results you will achieve. The most important point is to make what you do comfortable for you so that you will succeed. Whatever works best to that end is a good thing.

_____

_____

_____

_____

_____

_____

_____

_____

_____

_____

_____

_____

_____

_____

_____

_____

ACTION STRATEGY 9

THE 30-SECOND IMPRESSION

Like it or not, you sell. You sell yourself, you sell a product or you sell a service. If everyone is selling in the marketplace, then the question is "How do you sell in a way that's different than everyone else?" The way most people talk about their business is to talk about what they sell or the service they provide. "I sell computers." "I sell real estate." "I provide tax services or financial services." This type of selling adds no value, does not differentiate you, and candidly is pretty boring. You have seven to thirty seconds to make an impression and clearly and concisely describe your business in a way that someone else will want to ask you for a business card or want to get to know you better. In this section I am going to provide you with a template to craft a 30-second commercial, but how I do that will be quite different from what you might expect.

A thirty-second commercial is divided into three parts. Each part is ten seconds long. It's that simple.

The first part of the 30-second commercial begins with the purpose or the "why." Why are you doing what you do? What beliefs do you have that inspire and drive you to do things differently? Otherwise, all you did was take what you do and make a job for yourself working for yourself. In the seven clarities exercise you looked at what makes you unique. This is a great foundation to craft a sentence regarding what you believe about why your service or product impacts lives. See, if you are just selling another pen, you are just another pen salesman. If you just prepare tax returns, then you are just a tax return preparer.

The vision of our business is to tap into the tremendous potential that exists within businesses and families to build wealth and nourish legacy. Our mission is to change the way people think, and to talk about wealth not only in terms of money, but in values, beliefs, and traditions. The underlying reason for why we do what we do is that after 30 years of preparing plans for people, I realized that many times people ended up fighting over the plans. In litigation, families are being ripped apart, brothers and sisters stop talking, and money that could be invested in the family is wasted on frivolous lawsuits. If we as attorneys were doing such a good job, why were there so many lawsuits? I saw that most people coming into my office were coming in for a one-off transaction, not a long-term wealth-building relationship. In addition, the industry changed in the sense that the reason people came in for planning was to save taxes, but changes in the tax law took away this reason for most people. This change forced me to do some hard thinking about what this industry was really about. From this thinking I began to focus on a greater purpose that doing these plans represented. The plans were really a statement about family values and beliefs. They also represented how the family viewed its own readiness for wealth. Out of these ideas came the belief that everyone can have a legacy of their own choosing and one they like.

In another example, Apple Computer wanted to make computers accessible to the everyday person and give them a better computing experience. That's it. That was their purpose and motivation for creating the company they did, and everything that comes out of Apple is developed with the "why" in mind.

ACTION STEP

Why do you do what you do? What is your purpose for being in business and serving others?

_____

_____

_____

_____

_____

_____

_____

_____

_____

_____

_____

_____

The second part of the 30-second commercial moves to "how." What is the manner, environment, context, or experience in which you deliver your product or service? For Apple it was the layout of the computer, the sophistication of the design itself, and the process for how users interacted with the computer. In our company we have a nicely decorated office, a relaxing but professional atmosphere, and we use a combination of spoken and visual tools to introduce people to new ideas and possibilities of what they can do to build wealth.

ACTION STEP

Please take a few moments to write down the second 10 seconds of your 30-second commercial by describing the manner or environment, or anything special about how you want to provide your product or service.

_____

_____

_____

_____

_____

_____

The third part of the 30-second commercial is the "what." The "what" is your product or service. For Apple, the "what" is that they just happen to sell computers. In our company, we just happen to form legal entities, prepare wills and trusts, do tax planning, and manage money.

Please take a few moments and write down the "what" of your business.

_____

_____

_____

_____

_____

_____

_____

_____

_____

The last step is to put it all together. Here is our company's thirty-second commercial: We believe in tapping into the tremendous potential that exists in businesses and families to build wealth and nourish legacy by changing the way businesses and families think and talk about wealth, not only in terms of money, but in values, beliefs, and traditions. We show them how to overcome barriers, build wealth, and nourish legacy for generations. We do this by preparing wills and trusts, forming entities, tax planning, and money management.

Now Write Your Own 30-Second Commercial

_____

_____

_____

_____

_____

_____

_____

_____

_____

_____

_____

_____

_____

_____

_____

_____

_____

_____

_____

_____

_____

_____

_____

ACTION STRATEGY 10

BUILD A BRICK HOUSE

"Winning means fame and fortune.
Losing means certain death.
The Hunger Games have begun …"

From the movie *The Hunger Games*

In 2012, statistics from the U.S. Department of Commerce and the Department of Labor, among others, showed that 85% of businesses fail in the first year, 70% in the second year, 62% in the third year, 55% in the fourth year, and 50% in the fifth year. Kind of makes you wonder why anyone goes into business. Oh. Except everyone is in business in some way. If you are working for someone else, they have a business. And business is about making profits to sustain lives, because without business, people would have no work and no way to survive.

52% of businesses are home-based, and 63% of businesses have no employees.

Let me tell you a tale of three entrepreneurs: Steve Raw, Woodrow Woods (Woodie), and Bree Hicks. They dreamed their entire life of building wealth and nourishing legacy. The three entrepreneurs set out on their journey.

Before long, the three entrepreneurs came across Harold the Hamster. They asked Harold, "How do we build wealth and nourish legacy?" Harold replied, "You just keep running faster and faster and faster and faster, and you will get somewhere." The three entrepreneurs thanked Harold and continued on.

Soon they saw Susie the Salmon swimming upstream. "Susie, how do we build wealth and nourish legacy?" Susie said, "Live, spawn, and your life will be complete." The three entrepreneurs thanked Susie and continued on.

A little while later they ran into Larry the Lion. "Larry, how do we build wealth and nourish legacy?" Larry thought for a moment and roared, "Kill the competition."

The three entrepreneurs were grateful for the answers, but they were still not satisfied. So they sought out Oscar, the wise old owl. "Oscar, how do we build wealth and nourish legacy?" Oscar looked at the budding entrepreneurs and said "Whoooo. Whooooo wants to know?" "It is us, wise old Oscar. Steve Raw, Woodie, and Bree Hicks."

Oscar told them that there are sources of funds and uses of funds. A source of funds is something that is available to you. A use of funds is when someone else has control of your money. Part of building wealth and nourishing legacy is to make uses of funds into sources of funds and keep what you have earned.

At that moment Steve Raw jumped up and said, "I got it. I will set up my business as a sole proprietorship." The most common way business owners start a business is as a sole proprietorship. This simply means you are doing business on your own without any formal legal structure. To get started as a sole proprietorship, all you need is a business license and a bank account, and you can begin doing business. With a sole proprietorship, what you make less what you spend is your profit. That profit will be subject to tax. From a legal perspective, a sole proprietorship gives you no legal protection against creditors or lawsuits. This means that anything you own is at risk of being taken.

Without protection, Steve Raw was all alone. He had no protection. So the big bad creditors came and they huffed and they puffed and they blew his business down. The other two entrepreneurs watched in horror as their brother's business failed.

Woodie said, "I am not going to make that mistake. I am going to set up my business as a general partnership." The next way that two people might do business is in the form of a general partnership. A general partnership is simply two people coming together to do business. Like the sole proprietorship, a general partnership doesn't require much more than a business license and a bank account. Like the sole proprietorship, a general partnership gives you no legal protection against creditors and lawsuits. For this reason, most people do not form general partnerships as a way of doing business.

A general partnership usually is formed by agreement between the general partners. The partnership agreement will discuss who will contribute what assets to the partnership, how they will share profits and losses, who is responsible for management decisions, and more.

One of the problems that arises in doing business in a general partnership without a written agreement is when the partners want to go their separate ways or one of them passes away. Without an agreement, and mutual cooperation, the once friendly partners become rivals and oftentimes end up in court.

Woodie also went unprotected. Therefore the termite gang ate away the foundations of the business, and the big bad creditors huffed and they puffed and they blew his business down.

Bree Hicks couldn't believe what she had seen. Her brothers' businesses were failures, in bankruptcy, owed money to the IRS, and had no hope of keeping money. She was determined not to let that happen to her. She set up a corporation.

When done correctly, a corporation is separate from its owners, and the corporation will provide liability protection to its owners, called shareholders, against lawsuits and creditors.

To be protected from liability, the shareholders of a corporation must follow the procedures and formalities that go with being a corporation. The corporation must have a separate bank account. The shareholder owners must not mix personal and business income and expenses. Certain annual actions are required. If not done correctly, creditors can sue the owners directly in what is called piercing the corporate veil and hold the owners personally responsible for anything that happens in the company.

Bree was very successful. When the creditors came, they huffed and they puffed and they huffed and they puffed, but they couldn't blow her business down. She went on to keep her money not just for herself, but for her children, her grandchildren, and even her great grandchildren.

There are so many rules and regulations. There are so many laws. There are so many tax laws. There are so many business considerations. Over the past 30 years my day-to-day work has been to advise our clients on which choice is right for them, keeping it simple, but providing them with a clear picture of the risks and rewards, the advantages and disadvantages, and the benefits of doing the right planning with the right structure. For example, in almost every case when a person is doing business, the best structure is to have a corporation—more specifically a corporation known as an S corporation, which simply means that the corporation is taxed pursuant to a whole section of the Internal Revenue Code known as Subchapter S.

ACTION STRATEGY 11

THREE WAYS TO MAKE MONEY

"Brother, can you spare a dime?"
1932 musical *Americana*

I've Been Working on the Railroad
Princeton University compilation, 1898

Let's be clear on a few things.

- First, money itself is a piece of paper with coloring on it. That's it. Money has meaning only to the extent we determine what meaning we want to give it.

- Second, the amount of money you have or don't have is based on your value in the marketplace and the value you bring to others.

- Third, what value you have and what value you bring to others is in your control, and you have an incredible capability of doing more than you could ever realize. Simple examples that illustrate this point are people who go back to school later in life or change careers, maybe several times, before they find the type of work that ignites their passion and moves them to become major successes. The television show Shark Tank is also a great example of people who have had this experience. How many entrepreneurs started a business or came up with an idea after they lost their job or went through some type of challenge in their life? Whatever it is that excites you, figure out how you can make that more valuable, and the money will follow.

There are three ways to make money. Well, three legal ones, anyway.

The first way to make money is through a job or career. Labor hours. Trading dollars for hours of labor. In my view, a job or career is like lifting weights. There is nothing wrong with having a job or career if that is the choice you have made. However, I personally believe it is a hard way to make a living. It's a lot of work, and unless you keep doing it over and over and over again, the benefits are temporary. Doctors, lawyers, CPAs, if they aren't working the labor hours, they aren't making money. There is no recurring revenue, no mailbox money coming in as you sleep or go on vacation. Being in a career also has an inherent limitation in that it is difficult to reproduce yourself. Knowledge tends to be limited to your own. Years and years of study, learning, and doing. You can't really just hire someone and teach them all that knowledge. Unlike mass production of a product, taking a profession and scaling it or leveraging it to a bigger audience has its challenges.

The second way to make money is by owning investments. Investments generate income without you having to do the work. Dividends, interest, or rents. The goal of this book is to get you building wealth to the point that you have enough income so you don't have to work later on in life, or at the very least you have extra money for the fun things you like to do. Building a business is like creating an investment. Receiving a rate of return where you don't have to be doing all the work.

The third way to make money is by selling products. This is a really good way to make money, because now you have something tangible that you are making, something that can be systemized, something that can be scaled or mass-produced and sold, whether you are around or not.

Regardless of the way you make money, a key principle to accelerate your ability to make money is leverage. Leverage other people's skills, time, energy, and knowledge. This is one of the better ways to make money. Those in the real estate industry are masters at leverage. A real estate agency will acquire a broker's license and then hire many real estate agents to go out and sell real estate. Every time a sale is made, the real estate broker receives a portion of the commission.

ACTION
STEP

How are you going to make money?

_____

_____

_____

_____

_____

_____

_____

_____

ACTION STRATEGY 12

STAY OUT OF THE POORHOUSE

Building wealth and nourishing legacy means mastering the money we spend, the outflow of cash. Making money can be hard, but losing it can be very easy. Like the old saying "A fool and his money are soon parted."

Take a moment right now and list all the money that comes into your life. Now do the same thing for all of your expenses.

Every one of them. From the Starbucks coffee you buy to the penny that you leave lying on the ground. Did I just write that? A penny lying on the ground? (I am calling that an expense, because all you had to do was pick it up and you would have had one more penny of money.) Appendix 1 is an income and expense compass. If you have not already done so, please turn to the appendix and begin listing your income and your expenses.

What is the net result? Is more money going out than is coming in? Take a moment and do the following:

1. Cross out things you don't need. This includes Starbucks coffee, dinner at McDonald's, ordering pizza from Domino's, and so forth. When I think about money I spend, such as a pizza for $20, and then I think about how much chicken, beef, vegetables, and canned goods I could buy for $20 and how long that food would last, I appreciate the impact of my spending.

2. Line through and put a new number next to other expenses that you think you could reduce. Here is a marketing ploy I dislike. Buy one item, say for $5, or get two for $9. It seems that you are getting a great deal by purchasing the two items. Here's the hidden negative. Instead of spending $5, you are actually spending $9, and what we just determined is that if your expenses exceed your income, you are broke. The extra $4 is not saving you money; it's costing you money. Think about it from the perspective of retailers. They just made $9, not $5. That's more income, more sales in their

pocket. That's what they want. More money in. Believe me, it didn't cost them $4 to make the extra item that you bought. They made money. This might be a concept that is valuable to you the next time you go to the grocery store and you have a limited amount to spend. One exception I might make to this rule is an item like toilet paper that you are going to use all the time.

3. Think of substitutes for the items you have written down, and put new items next to them that wouldn't cost quite as much. Do you get the store-brand cereal or do you buy the more expensive brand? How about medicines? Do you get the generic or the brand label? Do you spend time finding coupons to save money?

The single most important goal is to make sure that more money is coming in than going out.

ACTION STRATEGY 13

MASTER BUDGET, MASTER YOU

"Do I not destroy my enemies when I make them my friends?"
—Abraham Lincoln

You may think that tracking income, expenses, budgeting, numbers and math is for the nerds and geeks. Maybe it's not one of your strong skills or best areas. However, building wealth and nourishing legacy requires knowledge of budgeting, and any good organization or department within it has a budget. Think of your family like a business. It has leaders, it produces activities, and it needs supplies on which to run. A budget is the company's income plan for the future. The budget will reflect what the company or family expects to make during a given time period, week, month, or year, and it also reflects the anticipated expenses. Having a budget will give a company a road map for sales to be made, goals to be met, and watching out to make sure not too much money is being spent. A budget is also very useful to compare how a company or family is actually performing against what was projected in the budget. The budget is written. Let me say that again, because this is important. The budget is written. It is not oral, not in one's head, not an idea, but in writing. How much money is expected to come in and how much money will you allow to go out? Let me say that again, because this is important. How much money will you allow to go out? The amount of money you allow to go out is up to you. You control you. You control your situation. You control the choices you make. You have the power to decide what money will go out. For example, if you are spending money on chips and eating out, you can control taking that money and buy food that is healthier and that will last longer.

In 2014, our company had one year left on the office lease. We had a choice. We could move to another space and most likely reduce our rent. The negatives were moving costs, printing costs for new stationery, the intangible costs of clients having to find the new space, furniture, and so much more. The new landlord most likely would have covered much of these costs through some free rent. The positives were staying put, not having business interruptions, and still being able to renegotiate the rent we were paying. We chose to stay put and to renegotiate the rent, and this negotiation saved us more than $1,000 a month. That's money that goes right into our pocket and makes us more profitable.

By making a budget, it is possible to measure reality against expectation. If expectations of income are too high, the company could go broke. If expectations of expenses are too low, the company could go broke. A budget can also be used as a goal-setting mechanism. Companies do this to increase sales, improve worker morale, and bind everyone together around a common cause.

Meeting a budget is gratifying. Not meeting a budget becomes a cause for concern. In our company, we have a budget. Every Monday morning we have a meeting to set priorities for where our team has to focus its efforts to maximize bringing in money. To give you an idea of how important this is, in the past we used to focus on work for clients who had the potential of making the highest dollars. The problem with this tactic, however, was that often the work for these clients took the longest not only in time, but also in terms of collecting money. That meant that our cash flow was tight and paying bills was even tighter. We decided to change our process to concentrate our efforts on work that could be done which would generate the most current or immediate revenue, while still working on projects that were longer term. This small change made a substantial difference in the cash flow we brought in each week to achieve our goals. We also created profit-sharing incentives for our team to motivate them to reach revenue targets.

In these last couple of chapters, I have provided you with some major weapons for use in overcoming barriers, building wealth, and nourishing legacy. Now it's your turn to use this information. Now it is your turn to make decisions on what money you want to come in and what money you will let go out. This will be your lifestyle plan. Take all of the expense items you wrote down and decide what you will spend more of, less of, substitute, or change around. Always keep in mind that the net result you want is a positive number. More money coming in than going out. This plan will act as your control and measuring stick. Every day, or week or month, record exactly the money coming in and the money going out. These are your actual numbers. Then measure the actual numbers against your plan. If there are discrepancies, then you can determine why and you can make decisions regarding how to change them. If the discrepancy is that you are bringing in more income than the plan, that is good. Put it into savings. If the discrepancy is that you are spending more money than in the plan, that is not good, and it needs to be changed or fixed. If the reason was an emergency, then you may need to take steps to allocate monies from other places to the emergency. You may need to work on saving a little more and putting it into an emergency fund.

One more comment. Many times people think they have to pay their bills the exact moment they come in. This is a false perception. The reason this is a false perception is that most of the time when all bills are paid exactly when they come in, then there is no money left over to save for yourself. When you have no money left over to save for yourself, then there is no way you will ever be able to build wealth. A different strategy is to make sure you put a small amount of money away every week or every month for yourself. When you do that type of saving, the small amount of money you put away can eventually grow to be used later for something you want or deem worthwhile. The bills that absolutely need to be paid each month should be paid. The bills that can wait a little longer without too much harm, you can delay paying. I want to make clear that I am not suggesting that you don't pay your bills. That's wrong, and it shows a lack of integrity. I am suggesting that by following the above strategy, you can simultaneously build wealth and take care of your needs and obligations.

ACTION STRATEGY 14

TOP TEN LIST

Many business owners go out of business because they fail to establish solid foundations for their business. Here are my top ten foundations for business that can make a significant difference in your success at building wealth.

1. THINK LIKE A BUSINESS OWNER

At the beginning of the book I talked about how it can take 10,000 hours of full-time work to get to mastery. Oftentimes, when people go into business, they lack experience. The lack of experience I am talking about, though, is not in performing one's craft; rather, it is the lack of experience in being a business owner. Thinking like a business owner is very different from simply working your craft in your business. Many times people start working for themselves because they are really good at a craft. The key words here are "working for themselves." They aren't running a business. What they have done is to create a job for themselves where they employ themselves. What happens in that situation is that the business owner ends up wearing many hats—sales, marketing, production, accounting, taxes. And with all these hats, the business owner finds himself or herself working 16-hour days and struggling just to make ends meet, all the while telling themselves they love what they do because they are working for themselves. Well, loving what you do may be the specific craft you were trained for, but running a business is a very different idea.

When you are running a business, you are managing people, you are creating a vision and purpose for the company, you are monitoring performance and growth. No longer are you sitting in your cave, so to speak, working your craft. Thinking like a business owner requires a whole different mindset than simply creating a job for yourself.

2. CAPITAL IS CRUCIAL

Simply put, not having enough capital means not having enough money set aside to last through the time necessary to build up sufficient sales to make the business successful. As we saw from earlier statistics, about 85% of businesses fail in the first year. This means they couldn't generate enough sales to cover the expenses they had to pay. When money out exceeds money in, it means you are broke.

Another viewpoint regarding lack of capital comes from Brian Tracy in his Universal Laws of Success and Achievement. He discusses the old adage that necessity is the mother of all invention. When a person has nothing to fall back on, they either succeed or perish. In those times, people become inventive and creative and find ways to make money. What Mr. Tracy is suggesting from this viewpoint is that it is the lack of capital that can fuel the fire of success. When a company has sufficient money to run and meet its needs, the urgency to complete goals may not be as strong and failure of the company could occur more rapidly. Consider the entrepreneurs who appear on *Shark Tank*. Those who had nothing to fall back on worked the hardest and were the most determined to succeed.

Given the choice, I would rather have some capital to fall back on in lean times or during unforeseen events. However, not having capital is a sure incentive to creativity, innovation, and plain old hard work to succeed.

3. LOCATION, LOCATION, LOCATION

This is never more true than in real estate. This is true for restaurants and I think other businesses in general. We have a shopping center in our neighborhood. (Who doesn't these days?) In this one center, there have been at least three or four different restaurant changes in one location. The center is a good center; it has fast food, a grocery store, a Target, a bookstore, computer store, juice stores, and more. Even though the center is a good and thriving one, the sit-down traffic needed to keep the one restaurant location in business just has not been sufficient. Location, location, location. Location in this center just doesn't work for a small independent restaurant.

On the other hand, down the block there is a soup and salad restaurant right next door to a tire company, across from a pharmacy and grocery store. It is not a fancy center, yet despite the seemingly less desirable business in this area, this soup and salad restaurant does a robust business. Location, location, location.

4. MANAGE BUSINESS RESOURCES

Imagine having customers wanting your product and you being unable to meet the demand. What do you think will happen to these customers? They will go elsewhere. That is lost sales and money out of your pocket. I have to buy tennis shoes every six months or so, and the last time I needed shoes, the company that I buy from didn't have my size in stock. I ended up finding another store on the Internet and bought from them. Worse, if you have too much inventory, then you have spent a lot of money to acquire that inventory, and the product sitting on the shelf is now going to waste because you can't make enough sales. That is a huge cost. I remember back when I was 16 in high school working at, yes, I admit it, McDonald's. I was acting as an assistant manager and was responsible for anticipating how many hamburgers would be needed for the lunch or dinner crowd rush. I would tell the cooks to prepare 12 Big Macs or 24 cheeseburgers, something like that. When the lunch or dinner crowd rush was over, part of my performance measurement was to look at how many burgers remained in the warming bin. If there was one or two, that was really good. If there were five or ten, that was not so good. For me, being the overachiever I am, it was kind of a game, but an important one. Aiming for perfection and settling for excellence was a good challenge for me.

5. CHOOSE PURCHASES CAREFULLY

A fixed asset is a piece of equipment that is used to make something. A simple example is a copy machine. If you spend too much money on the copy machines, furniture, or artwork used in your office or manufacturing plant, then that money is gone and can't be used for sales, marketing, production, or other revenue-generating activities. If the fixed assets aren't actually used in the revenue-producing activities of your business, that is like a double whammy against you. You are spending money on the equipment and you aren't producing any revenue from it, like the copy machine. If you are in manufacturing and you spend too much money on plant equipment, you could be in trouble if you can't generate the sales needed to support the equipment. I have seen this happen in printing businesses where the owner buys a really expensive digital printing machine, and then the amount of sales is insufficient to support the sophisticated printing that the machine can produce.

6. CREDIT CAN KILL

Leasing equipment or borrowing money on credit results in a monthly interest cost, and that monthly cost is critical to profit, because these are dollars that come straight out of your pocket. Until you are making at least enough money to match your expenses, you are in danger of going broke and failing. Higher interest rates are a pure cost of money. Debt and lease costs make you an employee beholden to the company you are leasing from or to whom you owe the debt. When was the last time you bought a car? Did you buy the car using the dealer's financing? Except for the occasional deal with zero percent financing, most of the time the finance cost is about 2–3%, unless you have bad credit, in which case it could be as high as 8% or more. How many months or years of the loan do you have to pay this cost? Four years, five years, or even seven years? Think about that. For four to seven years you have to work and be sure you make enough money just to pay this one debt to the automobile dealer. When you add to this amount rent or a mortgage payment, credit card debt, store credit card debt (the worst), credit for the television or stereo or furniture or clothes, and utilities, the amount of debt and expenses incurred can truly make you a slave—working for others to pay for the fun and toys you want.

7. AVOID CO-MINGLING OF FUNDS

If you are the sole owner of a business, it probably doesn't matter if you are taking money out of the company and using it for your personal purposes, unless that money was needed for the business. Determining a reasonable amount that should be put back as an investment in the business is an important consideration in planning for a business. Personal use of business funds can get a business in trouble in a way different than you might expect. When a business owner mixes business and personal funds in such a way that it is hard to tell them apart, there are two potentially devastating consequences. First, if there is a lawsuit, the people suing may go after the owner for personal liability in addition to the company itself. An example of this happening is when a person sets up a corporation or limited liability company to protect against personal lawsuits, but they fail to follow the right rules and formalities. This failure results in the ability of a potential creditor to "pierce the corporate veil" and go after the individual's assets. Second, if you mix personal and business income and expenses, the IRS may question the validity of the business expenses. If you can't justify them, you could end up paying more in taxes.

8. BEWARE RAPID GROWTH

One might consider this a good problem. The problem with unexpected growth, however, is that it can put a strain on the resources of the business, and if the business is unable to handle that growth, manage it, and improve the various components of the business needed to meet that growth, then the business can find itself out of business. It is also possible that the business simply doesn't have the right experience to handle the additional growth. In other words, if people have to be hired quickly to manage the growth and they haven't had the correct time and training, then mistakes will be made, customers can become unhappy, and the business's reputation may be tarnished and unrecoverable.

9. COMPETITION CREATES COMMODITIES

I went into law when I realized I wasn't going to become a doctor. Law wasn't my first choice, and it wasn't something I was driven to do at an early age. I came to enjoy tax law as a way to help people keep money in their pocket and away from the IRS. I also like that it is an area that is constantly changing. As a career, it has provided a decent living. In the year 2000, I saw the winds of change on the horizon. I knew that seven to ten years in the future, the tax law would radically change in a way that would reduce the amount of strategy and planning that could be provided by tax lawyers. This meant that the industry products, wills and trusts and other documents, were likely to become more of a commodity. And anytime there is a move toward commoditization, price gets reduced. Not coincidentally, this is the same time that the prepaid legal companies started. (Note: In my opinion the products delivered by these companies are so inferior that it ends up costing the consumer more to fix the problem, so beware.)

While the value of planning for taxes was diminishing, law schools were still churning out large numbers of lawyers. That meant fewer jobs for more lawyers who had to find a way to make money. Making money meant these lawyers were willing to cut prices, particularly if they were working out of their homes, making competition even tougher. In today's world, virtual offices are becoming more common. This certainly helps lower costs, but it also means there are more pools of talent in the marketplace, thereby creating more competition.

The winds of change are always blowing. As a business owner, one of the best things you can do is to always be on guard, thinking about and forecasting changing trends in your industry, the market in which you serve, the economy or the society. This doesn't necessarily mean your company needs to always be shifting with the change, but it does have to be ready when a substantial change occurs that can impact your business, whether negatively or positively.

10. SALES SOLVES PROBLEMS

It has been said that sales solves all problems. As we saw at the beginning of this book, however, if the money isn't managed correctly or the mindset isn't right, then just having sales isn't the total answer. With more sales does come more money. Depending on the cost to produce those sales, taxes, and other expenses, it may not be a lot of money, but it is more money nonetheless. The question of how much money you keep will be left to a later tip.

There are many different sales techniques. Business owners often get confused and mix up steps in the selling process. I want to focus on one technique that helped change my understanding of business and how we now approach sales in our company.

The technique comes from one of the top sales trainers in the world. His name is Eric Lofholm of Eric Lofholm International, and the technique is called the Unstoppable Sales System, which features the sales mountain. In the sales mountain metaphor, Eric talks about how each business owner is a guide leading clients and prospects up a sales mountain. Guides bring people from one place to another with a purpose. In the sales mountain, the role of the guide is to lead a prospect or customer up the mountain to the goal of making a sale. (Note: I am a trainer in Mr. Lofholm's company and am authorized to sell the Unstoppable Sales System.)

GENERATE A LEAD

The first step up the sales mountain is to get more leads. In business, developing a lead-generating system is crucial. Some businesses will have five, ten, or more lead-generating systems. There is only one purpose to generating leads and a lead generation system. That purpose is to get more leads. That's it. There is no other purpose for this first step.

What are some ways leads are generated?

1. Going to a networking event and getting a business card.

2. Having lunch with a strategic referral partner.

3. Having a way to ask clients for more referrals.

4. Sending out letters, coupons, and sample products.

The guy with the biggest database wins. It costs more to obtain a new customer than to get a present customer to buy more of what you have to sell. The more leads, fans, and community in your database, the easier it is to sell to them.

When I heard this concept, what became clear to me is why I was so unsuccessful at networking events in the past. I did not have the right understanding for my purpose in going to these events. I used to look for people I knew, was comfortable with and could talk with, and avoid the people I really didn't want to meet, whose only interest was to throw a business card at me, tell me everything they do, and who have no real interest in hearing about my business or what I enjoy. After the event, I deceived myself into thinking I was doing networking, with the result that I placed the collected business cards into the proverbial circular file (trash can). When I realized that the purpose of a lead generation system is only to generate leads, my thinking completely changed. Now when I go to an event, I am less concerned with the thought of establishing deep relationships or learning every detail of a person's business. Rather, I focus on who might be the top three people I want to get to know better, have a brief discussion, and obtain their information for a later connection.

What's your purpose for attending an event? If your purpose is simply to get leads, then you should be less concerned with anything else. One additional point on this topic is that if your sole purpose is to generate leads, then spending lots of time talking to any one person will defeat that purpose. However, there is a balance between good conversation and being too abrupt. Just something to keep in mind as you move forward in this part of the sales mountain.

I bet you know what is coming now. You get to take some time and write down ways you can think of simply to generate leads. I am not talking about what to do with them once they are generated. Just ways to generate a lead.

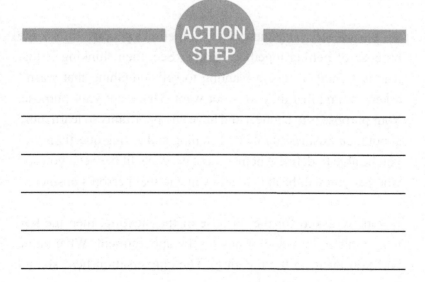

ACTION STEP

_____

_____

_____

_____

_____

SET AN APPOINTMENT

After the lead generation step comes the second step in the sales mountain, which is appointment setting. Once you have attended the networking event and you have obtained leads, the next step is to determine what you will do with the stack of leads you have collected. Other than putting them in your database for future emails, social media, newsletters, etc., the next step is to select which people you want to establish a connection with and make an appointment. Once you have made this decision, then you get to do one really tough task. Pick up the telephone and make a call to that person and set an appointment. That's it, because the whole purpose of setting an appointment is to set an appointment. Nothing more. In setting an appointment, you aren't selling. You aren't convincing the person of how great you are. All you are doing is saying, "I want to get to know you better. Can we have a chance to do that?"

People are very busy these days. Sometimes people will ask the purpose of getting together. Really? See, their thinking is that it is just another person wanting to sell something that wasn't asked for and that they may not want. That's not your purpose. Your purpose is to connect and have an opportunity to learn more about their business. Only by listening and asking questions will you be able to define whether there is even a fit between you and whether you will be able to add value to that person's business.

If you are asked for the purpose of the meeting, then the key is to explain the value of having the appointment. What value will you bring to the meeting? The conversation here should be focused on them, not you. One response might be simply, "Because I wanted to get to know you better, learn more about your business, and whether there may be some common ground and value in working together."

In a mastermind group in which I am involved, I mentioned that I was looking for certain strategic relationships in our industry. I was introduced to a business attorney who had formed a small group of attorneys consisting of himself, a real estate attorney, and a litigation attorney. These areas of practice are all complementary and noncompetitive with my practice area. We had lunch, we talked about what we were doing for our practices, and from those brief meetings, we have begun to refer business to each other. The point of setting an appointment was to set an appointment and get to know each other.

When you set an appointment, have in mind some very specific ideas of what you want to accomplish in that appointment. Make it a productive meeting and do not waste the other person's time.

ESTABLISH TRUST AND RAPPORT

Once the appointment is set, the next part of the sales mountain is where we really begin to make the ascent to the top. I know what you may be thinking. "Now that I have the appointment set, I have my chance to talk about all the things I can do to help the person." *Buzzzzz.* Wrong answer. I don't know how many times I have a meeting with someone and they show up, and as I call it, throw up. They talk only about themselves, how great their product is, and why we should do business with them, even though they are selling water slides and we live near the beach.

When you get together for an appointment, the first objective of the meeting should be to establish trust and rapport. Find common ground—people, places, likes, or dislikes that give you commonality to talk about. It has been said that people will do business with people they like and trust. This is partially true. People will do business with people they like and trust provided the person can satisfy the primary customer's wants or needs. If you can satisfy a client's wants or needs, they don't have to like you. If they like you but you can't satisfy their needs and wants, they won't buy from you. If you can satisfy their needs and wants and they like you, you are golden, and you will have a customer for a long time.

One word of caution here. Be genuine and authentic. Attempting to establish trust and rapport in a superficial way will fail. I have been in meetings where I was asking questions about a person's background or family, and I realized the person across the table just wanted to do business. I would stop and move on to the topic at hand, because the meeting wasn't about me; it was about the customer.

One time my family and I were in a store shopping for furniture. The kids were about ten at the time. This one unlucky sales guy approached us. At the time I wasn't really in the mood to talk to a salesperson anyway, so here is this guy and one of the first words out of his mouth was, "You have great kids." Now, in retrospect I know I was being a bit harsh, but all I could think about was how the heck did he know anything about my kids? His attempt to establish trust and rapport in this way was almost an affront to me, using the kids to get through to us. He did not read me well at all.

For salespeople at stores, I know this is a difficult situation. This is why I like compensation-based salespeople, not commission-based ones. By receiving a wage, the salesperson can be truly interested in making sure the customer's needs are satisfied, not in seeing how another sale can be made for the benefit of the salesperson. It's an inherent conflict of interest that can be an obstacle. For me personally, when I am shopping, I like it when someone simply comes up, introduces themselves, and says, "If there is anything you need or I can be of help, just let me know." That's it. For people who want to look around, it's not intrusive. People who want to open up a bit and further the conversation will do so. Everyone's style is different and everyone's needs are different. There is no good way to find the right trust and rapport. However, it's amazing how I have met people with seemingly nothing in common, only to find out that we grew up in the same neighborhood, our kids have the same birthday, or something small that creates a little smile and light on our face when we find something to talk about.

FIND THE CUSTOMER'S NEED

Once trust and rapport have been established, the fourth step up the sales mountain is the most crucial. This step could lead you further up the mountain or plunge you off the cliff. This step is to ask questions and find the customer's pain. What challenges might they be having? What people do they want to meet? How do they solve a problem they are having? Only by listening to the other person and asking what is important to them will you even begin to frame how you can be of value. Like the old adage, "God gave us two ears and one mouth." There probably was a reason for that.

We have a simple system in our company. We make it clear that the purpose of the first meeting is an assessment so we can get to know the person, understand their concerns, and obtain the facts. Only then will we begin to discuss ideas or strategies that might be suitable for them. Of course, at the initial part of the meeting we will establish trust and rapport by asking the customer to tell us a little bit about themselves. If the client came from a referral, that is usually a good starting point. After the strategy session, we will let the client know that we will prepare a plan for them containing the steps to meet their needs. Last, we will implement the parts of the plan that the client wishes to implement.

I had a client who had been doing business with us for around eight years. He wanted us to do another project, and when I quoted him the price, he balked. He knew our value, but he was the kind of guy to whom negotiating price was important. I didn't want to come down on price, and he suggested he might seek other attorneys to do the job. At the tipping point, I asked some questions about his top limit. He told me, and I agreed. I wasn't stupid. I didn't want to lose him as a client, and now we have an even better relationship, where his trust in me extends to other areas of his life and the life of his entire family. What could be more gratifying?

There is a whole body of material on different sales techniques, which is beyond the scope of this book. Each of these sales principles deals with how we show up in the selling process and how what we do can improve or wreck a sale.

BENEFITS, BENEFITS, BENEFITS

Once you have identified the real needs and pains of the customer, then you get to use the best part of the selling process. This is the part where you get to explain the benefits of your product or service and how these benefits will resolve a customer or prospect's concerns. Eskimos probably don't need ice. A person moving into town most likely will need new gardeners, or dentists, doctors, lawyers, financial advisors, cleaners, or places to eat, and the list goes on. What benefits do you have to offer your customer or prospect, and what makes them unique?

_____

_____

_____

_____

_____

SUMMIT THE OFFER

The sixth step in the sales mountain is the summit. This is where you make the sales offer. If we have established good trust and rapport, found out the customer's pain, and determined how our product or service can address that pain, then we get to ask the customer or prospect whether they would like to move forward and do business. Asking for the sale should be the simplest part of the sales mountain. If the hard work has been done during the climb, then that last little step to get to the sale should fall into place.

Sometimes in the process we hit obstacles or objections, and our job is to overcome these objections. Most common objections are formed around price, time, and quantity. There are substantial resources discussing how to overcome objections that are beyond the scope of this book.

To summarize, we begin climbing the mountain by generating leads. With leads in hand, we begin to build our database and look to set appointments with those leads. The purpose of setting an appointment is to set an appointment. The key to setting an appointment is strictly to talk about the value of the appointment. Once the appointment is set, the first part of the meeting is to establish trust and rapport and find people, places, likes and dislikes in common. Just about everyone has something in common in some way. With good trust and rapport, asking questions to find customer needs and pain is the essential part of climbing the mountain. Do it well, and the peak is in sight. Do it poorly, and you might just fall off the mountain. With customer pain or needs in mind, the opportunity to explain the benefits of your product or service are at your fingertips, and once the benefits are explained, you get to ask for the sale. Sometimes customers might object, and knowing how to respond to those objections is very important. Through this give and take and back and forth, if the customer pain is large enough and you have shown enough value in solving that pain, closing the sale will be achieved.

ACTION STRATEGY 15

PAY YOURSELF FIRST

When it comes to investing, "Pay yourself first" is a golden rule. If you don't pay yourself first, how are you supposed to build wealth? If you make money and pay all your debts and spend it on short-term benefits, there is no money left over to save for the future. The rule of thumb is that you should have at a minimum six months' worth of salary in the bank in the event something unexpected happens. Here is what happens when you don't pay yourself first. Your paycheck comes in. You pay the rent or mortgage. You pay the car payment, insurance, and utilities. You pay the credit card for gas, meals, and going out to a restaurant with the family. You pay for groceries and so forth. After you are done paying for all of this, you have nothing left, and you wait until the next paycheck.

When you pay yourself first, here is what the process looks like. You get your paycheck and you decide on some amount to put into a savings account, maybe even an investment account. Let's say you decide to make it 5% of what you make, or even $100. Now you go to pay all the bills. You realize you may not have quite enough, so you decide that you can wait on paying the utility bill for a couple of weeks because it won't cost you anything. You might also delay the doctor bill or some other bill where there is no penalty. (I am not suggesting you don't pay your bills. I always pay my bills, but sometimes you can delay payments without consequences, and this can allow you to put money away for yourself.) Now you have $100 in the bank. The next paycheck comes and you pay yourself first, and then you pay the bill you were holding off paying. You might cut down on a few cafe lattes and use that extra money to pay an expense or two. As you do this with each paycheck, month after month, all of a sudden you will have saved $600, $1,000, or more, and you're meeting all of your obligations. That feels good, and you want more. You pick up money on the ground because it's FREE. That adds to your savings. You save your change. It's yours to keep. If you invest this money, you may start to make money on that money. IT DIDN'T COST YOU ANYTHING TO DO THAT.

The timing and amounts of how much you make in investments will vary, but steady wins the race. As you build money, if an emergency comes along, you will have comfort in knowing that you have money saved to take care of life's unexpected moments.

As you continue saving, you realize that you might be able to avoid putting money on credit cards. Credit cards are evil. They trap you in chains of the future, and that future is someone else's, not yours. How many times do we promise ourselves that we will pay the credit card on time and in full? Then when the time comes to pay the bill, something else comes up, which we take care of, realizing that we can just pay the minimum on the credit card. Once this spiral starts, interest on the unpaid debt starts accruing, and then we have to work harder and harder to pay someone else. Get rid of the credit cards and you will be on your way to saving money. It is suggested that concentrating on paying off one card can be beneficial, and I agree with this idea. Get rid of one debt, then use the extra money to concentrate on getting rid of a second debt. The extra money will pay down the debt faster. You can also make a small extra payment before the due date and reduce how much interest is charged. While you continue to pay yourself first, you will build wealth while you are taking care of your other obligations. At some point in the future you will achieve your goal, pay the debt, and have money to spare. PAY YOURSELF FIRST is the golden rule. Start Now.

ACTION STEP

Determine a comfortable amount of money that you can put into the bank from each paycheck or the money you receive from products or services, and do so. Then look at all your other expenses and determine the highest-priority ones, pay them, and keep paying all other expenses until your bank balance is $50. At this moment, stop paying any more bills, because you always want to have a little cash in the bank. Each month repeat the process.

★ Complete

ACTION STRATEGY 16

THE FALLACY OF THE RULE OF 72

Albert Einstein reportedly said that the most powerful force in the universe is compound interest. Compound interest means that when you make an investment and that investment earns interest, in each future year the interest earned continues to be added to the original investment, plus the interest that was made previously.

The rule of 72 is a concept that reflects this principle. The rule of 72 allows you to determine how fast you can double your money given a certain rate of interest and a certain time period. As an example, if I take $100 and invest it at an interest rate of 10%, I can expect that in 7 years my $100 will double in value. (72 divided by 10 is roughly 7.) Here is the calculation. 100 becomes 110. 110 adds 11 to become 121. 121 adds 12 and becomes 133. 133 adds 13 and becomes 146. 146 adds 14 to become 160. 160 adds 16 to become 176. 176 adds 17 to become 193.

The rule of 72, when combined with paying yourself first, can be powerful. Each time you put money in the bank, interest begins to build on the amount you put in plus the interest you earn on each amount. Over time, the growth works to your advantage. If you put money into the stock market, then you can begin to determine from the investments you make what kind of return you can expect.

A simple example will help illustrate this concept. If you start with $100 and never add more money to it, and you earn an 8% rate of return on that money, it will take 9 years for the $100 to become $200. See Appendix 2 for the calculation on this. However, if you added $120 to this money every year, then over the same 9 years and with an 8% return, you would have $1,698.41, as is shown by the chart in Appendix 3.

Despite the benefits of compound interest and the rule of 72, here is the fallacy of the rule of 72. It assumes that one can earn a constant rate of return every year. This is downright unrealistic. This point is critical, because when I talk about building wealth, if there is a year in which wealth is destroyed by investing badly in the stock market, the time to recover that loss can take years. For example, if you have $100 invested and you suffer a 20% loss, down to $80, it takes a 25% increase on the $80 just to get back to even. Remember the Couch Potato and how starting early in investing can make a huge difference? Having a bad year late in life can devastate the assets built up, and that can severely impact the kind of lifestyle one desires. The importance of these points is that many people think they can just put some money into an investment account and the financial advisor will double their money based on the rule of 72. Since we have seen this is a fallacy, it is imperative to use the Pay Yourself First rule and realize that with this strategy and by being careful how you invest your money, you will give yourself the best chance of success in building wealth.

ACTION
STEP

Test it for yourself. From the money you set aside each month, figure out the interest rate or return you are receiving. Divide that into 72 and determine how long it will take for your money to double and how much you will have. If you like the results, congratulations; you are on your way toward building wealth and achieving the legacy of your dreams. If you do not like the results, then it's time to make changes in your life. Some of these changes might include cutting back on feel-good expenses like the Starbucks coffee or the money spent on lunch each week. Our company is uniquely positioned to review and analyze your lifestyle plan, financial and tax planning, and get you on track to building wealth.

_____

_____

_____

_____

_____

_____

_____

_____

_____

_____

_____

_____

_____

ACTION STRATEGY 17

CASH FLOW IS KING

Cash flow is the lifeblood of the business. Bills come in, and they must be paid. If there is not enough cash flow, the business won't have enough money to pay the bills and could go out of business. Many times, business owners confuse sales with cash flow. You can make a million dollars in sales, but if the money doesn't actually get paid, you have nothing. For business owners, cash flow is about what is in the bank and how much exists in client accounts receivable. Accounts receivable show how much in sales have yet to be collected from clients. A large accounts receivable can damage your business. The longer someone takes to pay you, the worse it is for you. And of course if they fail to pay you completely, you have rendered a service or provided a product that you could have sold to someone else.

The profit and loss statement is a great tool for looking at where the best revenue in your company is coming from and where you are incurring the most expenses. Each service or product line can be tracked to determine the best sellers and the most profit.

For example, if you know that your product is only making 10 cents for every product sold, you can then make good decisions on whether to simply increase the price of the product, assuming competition will allow for it, or whether you will have to sell more of the product to make more money.

Here is a story that further illustrates how cash flow is king. I had a client who made about half a million dollars per year and told me they had no money left over for themselves. Of course, it was hard to figure out how that could be, until I saw the profit and loss statement. The statement showed that about 90% of the revenue from the business was going to pay compensation to employees or independent contractors. That left 10% to pay all of the other company expenses. No wonder there wasn't any money left. This business was on life support.

One of my strengths as a tax lawyer is in being able to quickly look at the financial statements of a business and see where there are challenges and where improvements can be made, both from a business perspective and a tax perspective.

ACTION STEP

What is your cash flow on a daily, weekly, and monthly basis? Check your accounts receivable. That's money that could be in your hands, being put to good use for you. Are there changes that you might be able to implement to increase cash flow right now?

_____

_____

_____

_____

_____

_____

_____

_____

ACTION STRATEGY 18

BEWARE THE TAX DEMONS

Tax Demon Number 1:
The Self-Employment Tax

What you make from your work or your business is ordinary income, and it is subject to income tax at the highest rates. Period. If you are on the hamster wheel of sales, "make more, make more," in tax terms it's "tax more, tax more." If you are self-employed, which means you have created a job for yourself doing what you are good at, you get the additional privilege of paying a self-employment tax of about 15% on your net profit. Net profit is defined as the income you make less the expenses you pay. Here is an example. If you make $100,000 and you have expenses of $50,000, your net profit is $50,000 and you will pay a self-employment tax of how much? ($7,500) Do not pass go, do not collect $200. There is no escaping this tax. Now on the $50,000 you made, you also have to pay income taxes. It's possible that if you own a home and you have mortgage interest or property taxes, or you make charitable contributions, or you have college tuition, you may be able to reduce those income taxes, but you cannot escape the self-employment tax. At Legacy Legal, we help you avoid the tax demon of the self-employment tax.

Tax Demon Number 2:
The Phase-outs

I am not going to get into great detail on this one. Suffice it to say that if you start making too much money, certain deductions are reduced or phased out and you don't get them. This of course means you get to pay more taxes.

Tax Demon Number 3:
The Wealth Taxes

These taxes are designed to get you to pay more money just because some politician said so. Imagine you are in school. You study hard. You get an A. The teacher says, "Good job, Billy. I am going to give your A to Johnny, the person who didn't study and goofed off the entire class. Billy, you get a B." I don't know too many people other than Johnny who would be happy with this outcome, but this is exactly what is happening in the world of American politics and taxes in the years 2008–2015.

Tax Demon Number 4: The Alternative Minimum Tax

This tax is just like it sounds. It's an alternative tax and it is a minimum tax. That means that when you make a certain amount of money, if the regular tax is too low, the alternative minimum tax makes sure you pay more.

The tax demons can pillage your hard-earned money. I want you to avoid these taxes and put more money into your pocket. I have been in the tax law business for 30 years, working with clients on avoiding these tax demons. I want an opportunity to work with you and to see you on your way to building wealth and nourishing your legacy.

ACTION STEP

⭐ Call for a free 30-minute consultation regarding your business or personal tax situation.

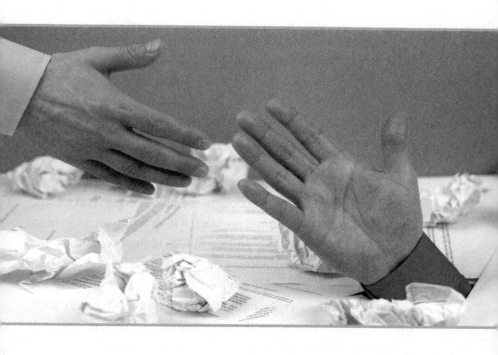

ACTION STRATEGY 19

FIND YOUR TAX ANGELS

Tax Angel Number 1:
The Tax Deferrals

Tax deferrals are strategies that allow you to defer paying taxes until a future date. These strategies include individual retirement accounts, simple and self-employed retirement accounts, 401k's, and annuities. These tools allow you to make investments, increase your wealth, and not pay taxes until you are older—70½, to be exact.

IRAs are a contract between the participant owner, the company managing the assets inside the retirement account, and a named beneficiary. IRA proceeds are not subject to probate.

Regular (traditional) IRA accounts are tax deferred, and by age 70½ the owner is required to start withdrawing money from the IRA, at which time it will be taxed. If the owner dies, the beneficiary has several options on how to receive money from the IRA. In many cases, I advise that beneficiaries choose the option where they can continue to take money out over their lifetime, which allows the IRA to continue to grow tax deferred, and only the income withdrawn is subject to taxation.

With tax deferrals you are saving money on a tax-deferred basis which is only to be used when you are done working. When you stop working, you will then start pulling money out of the tax-deferred vehicle to pay for your lifestyle, and at that time you will have to pay tax on the amounts withdrawn. The theory is that you won't need as much money in "retirement" for your lifestyle, and so you pay less tax on that deferred money than had you paid tax when you were working. In practice, this theory has not worked out too well, as most people's lifestyles are the same as when they were working. They are still paying the same high taxes on the money they have deferred. Still, the amount of growth that occurs in these accounts can last the remainder of a person's lifetime. Tax deferrals are a good tax strategy.

I have found that when people have no debt from paying off their mortgage, they are receiving social security, and have few healthcare costs because of Medicare, the money saved in the tax-deferred accounts will last them the rest of their lives. With all the bad news about healthcare and cost of living, this does provide some shining ray of hope for people and their future.

Tax Angel Number 2: The Tax Preferrals

Tax preferral strategies allow you to take deductions without ever having to pay for them. Examples include tax rate differences and a mileage allowance (if you drive a car for business purposes, you can take a deduction of about 55 cents per mile, provided you keep track of the miles driven). It's a pretty good deal. Another example is that when you buy equipment like a copy machine, or you buy rental real estate, you get to take a deduction every year. That's another free strategy that is pretty good. In some cases, such as buying equipment, you can take an immediate deduction for the full cost of the equipment, which reduces your income for tax purposes.

Tax Angel Number 3: The After-Tax Freebies

The after-tax freebies are a bit of a mixed blessing, but the long-term benefits are incredible. With the after-tax freebies, tax must first be paid on money that is made, but then that money is put into investments that are forever tax-free. The investments grow tax-free, the money never has to be taken out, and if the money is taken out, it is tax-free. Over the long term this strategy is the best at building wealth, because what is made over the long term more than makes up for the initial taxes that had to be paid.

Some of the strategies in the after-tax freebie camp are the Roth IRA, or Roth 401k, life insurance, and municipal bonds. By the way, if an investment is made in a stock and it's never sold, no taxes ever have to be paid. This is like the story of grandma and grandpa who gave Disney stock to their one-year-old, and by the time the child was forty, he or she was a millionaire.

Investing with the idea of not having to use the money is a great way to think about a legacy for children and grandchildren.

Tax planning is not for amateurs. With over 30 years of experience and an advanced degree in tax law, I work with clients all the time finding ways to avoid taxes and invest their money in tax-favored ways, putting more money into their pocket and helping them to build wealth and nourish legacy.

ACTION STEP

Are you using any of the tax deferrals, tax preferrals, or after-tax freebies?

_____

_____

_____

_____

_____

★ Call for a free 30-minute consultation regarding your business or personal tax situation.

ACTION STRATEGY 20

GOOD IS THE ENEMY OF GREAT

Good is a state of mind. Great is a state of mind. Which would you rather be? In his book, *Good to Great*, Jim Collins says the vast majority of companies never become great precisely because the vast majority of companies become quite good. That is their main problem. They get quite good, and they then settle and stop taking the actions necessary to become great.

What is the difference between good and great? Well, the word "good" is defined as sufficient or average, whereas "great" is defined as remarkable, exceptional, or outstanding.

Often we'll get to a point where we are quite good. We are seeing results and our finances are better than when we started, so we settle; we stop pushing for more and striving to be better. We stop pushing because we become good, even though we are not yet great. If you truly want to be great, then the mindset of "good is never enough" is absolutely critical.

Here is an important distinction. There is a vast difference between always wanting to be better versus nothing ever being good enough. Wanting to be better means you keep progressing. You don't quit. Nothing ever being good enough is a reason or excuse to stop, because you only see that your ability or performance isn't yet where it needs to be. You have to be able to look at the big picture and realize there is always room to reach higher, that there is always room for improvement. It doesn't mean you have to critically analyze every single micro detail of everything you are doing in order to become great.

In the world of business, especially that of entrepreneurship, and in most aspects of life, the ones who typically are most successful are those who are able to achieve that extra something, the ones who give that extra push, when everyone else has given up or settled.

Andre Agassi in his book *Open* describes how he hit millions of tennis balls as a child on his way to becoming one of the greatest tennis players of all time. He described how a little touch, a little flick, could make all the difference between winning and losing a point.

ACTION
STEP

★   What are you good at?

★   What should you be great at?

★   Are you settling for good?

★   How could you make your company great?

_____

_____

_____

_____

_____

_____

_____

ACTION STRATEGY 21

NOURISH LEGACY THROUGH LEADERSHIP

We are all leaders in some way. Leaders in our business, leaders of our family, leaders of others in groups or networks. Jim Collins, a professor at the University of Colorado at Boulder, identified 13 different types of leaders, which I have reproduced below. Naturally, everyone might have multiple characteristics, but usually one is predominant. No one type of leader is right or wrong. Different styles work for different people and different organizations. I have seen owners of companies who are brutal to their employees, and the employees take it for fear of losing their job, their own self-worth issues, or whatever the case may be. I have also seen leaders of companies who get the best out of their people. In the long run, these companies are usually the ones that last and go on to become leaders of their industries.

Charismatic

Charismatic leaders are incredible motivators with an enormous ability to influence others. As their influence grows, they tend to suck up oxygen, and their reigns tend to be cultlike.

Examples: Theodore Roosevelt and Jack Welch

Authentic

Authentic leaders are guiding beacons of constancy and discipline with integrity and character who take time to reflect. Shooting stars, by comparison, rocket to the top with no time to reflect or deepen.

Example: James Goodnight of the software giant SAS

Mindful

Mindful leaders pay attention, notice, probe, analyze, and listen to others and the environment within which they operate.

Example: A.G. Lafley of Procter and Gamble

Servant

Servant leaders wash each other's feet. They serve first, then lead so as to serve better.

Example: Herb Kelleher of Southwest Airlines

Storytelling

Storytelling leaders are usually entrepreneurs whose stories are their own.

Examples: Steve Jobs and Richard Branson

Adaptive

Adaptive leaders rise above the noise to interpret dynamic situations, adjust their values to changing circumstances, and then help people stretch to meet the unfamiliar without sacrificing their trust.

Example: Alan Mulally of Ford

Tribal

Tribal leaders have a sense of shared values, beliefs united under a common culture.

Example: Nick Swinmurn, founder of Zappos

Level 5

Level 5 leaders bestow credit generously, shoulder blame responsibly, and put the organization before self.

Example: Darwin Smith, former CEO of Kimberly-Clark

Resonant

With resonant leaders, morale rises and falls with the mood of the leader.

Example: Colleen Barrett of Southwest Airlines

Emotionally Intelligent

Emotionally intelligent leaders are aware of their own feelings and the feelings of others.

Example: Warren Buffett of Berkshire Hathaway

Strengths-Based

Strengths-based leaders identify and invest in their own and their employees' talents. Do you influence or are you a superb strategic thinker?

Examples: Simon Cooper, former CEO of Ritz-Carlton
Wendy Kopp, Teach for America

No-Excuse

No-excuse leaders are mentally tough and accountable.

Example: Brace Barber, U.S. Army Elite Ranger

Narcissistic

Narcissistic leaders don't listen, don't learn, don't teach, don't brook dissent.

Example: Bill Gates of Microsoft

While Bill Gates is mentioned above, it has been noted that he is a productive narcissist who thrives in turbulent times and attracts followers with compelling visions.

ACTION STEP

What kind of leader are you? What kind of leader do you want to be? List the traits and characteristics that make you a leader. What are your strengths and weaknesses as a leader?

_____

_____

_____

_____

_____

CONCLUSION

I would like to share a story of two daughters, a father, and a mother. The father was a certified public accountant who had a practice in Los Angeles. He and his wife were frugal and had a modest investment account. One daughter lived in San Diego and the other in Michigan. The two daughters weren't very close. Dad had passed away ten years earlier than Mom, and Mom was now beginning to have some memory challenges. The daughter in San Diego and her husband moved in with Mom to help care for her. The daughter in Michigan was a bit concerned about what her sister was doing and kept in contact. The daughter in San Diego and her husband had health issues, and the husband did not work. The daughter in Michigan had health issues and had just enough to make ends meet.

When Mom passed away, the daughters and I met to discuss the inheritance that the daughters would receive and the daughters' own living needs. At our first meeting, it became clear that the daughters were able to put away their ego, they became closer, and they wanted to make sure their lives were a bit easier and more stable. They did not have much experience with financial investments or lifestyle plans, but they were willing to begin the education process to become better masters of it. The daughters were open to the idea of receiving advice on strategies for building wealth.

They prepared a lifestyle plan for the money coming in from their work, social security, and pension, and they measured how much money was being spent. We reviewed the information for places where savings could occur. We looked at the future expectations of income and prepared a plan for building wealth. We discussed the behavior barriers of each daughter and how they approached money and the disciplines they needed to keep from spending the inheritance that the parents had worked so hard to give them. The daughters were grateful that their parents were able to leave them "something to make life just a bit easier," as they expressed in their words.

The daughter in Michigan moved out to California and found a place to settle within the lifestyle plan budget she prepared.

The daughter in San Diego found a wonderful place to live in Ramona, California. The parents' home was sold and the proceeds were invested. The daughters were given certainty and security, and will be in a position to succeed for the remainder of their life.

You too can succeed at overcoming barriers, building wealth, and nourishing a legacy. Start this journey. Learn to aim for perfection and settle for excellence. Adopt a mindset of mastery, get control over your ego, enjoy a different relationship with money, be in a job you like, or own a business. Develop a plan, being clear on what is important to you. Create a budget, be disciplined, and put money into investments on a regular and continuous basis. Keep money as a source of funds, take advantage of tax strategies, and be a good leader. Build your wealth and nourish your legacy.

We want you to stay engaged with us. This book is a first step. Our company has a Quick Start Guide that takes you into even greater depth in the Mind Money Strategies and many more. You can access this Quick Start Guide at www.mindmoneystrategy.com. We also have an advisor program for ongoing coaching and support each week. We offer seminars with exercises and games that get across lessons in a fun and interactive environment. You can also find out more about these seminars at www. mindmoneystrategy.com. We have a Facebook group for our members to stay engaged with each other. Please like us and share our posts. Thank you for your interest in *The Magic of Money*. I wish you the best of success in overcoming your barriers, building your wealth, and nourishing your legacy.

APPENDIX 1

INCOME AND EXPENSE COMPASS

Husband

Earned Income $_____
Interest/Dividends $_____
Business Income $_____
Social Security $_____
Pension $_____
Rental/Partnership $_____
Other Income $_____

TOTAL $_____

Wife

Earned Income $_____
Interest/Dividends $_____
Business Income $_____
Social Security $_____
Pension $_____
Rental/Partnership $_____
Other Income $_____

TOTAL $_____

Combined Income $_____

Estimated Expenses   (MONTHLY)

Rent/Mortgage $_____
Property taxes $_____
Utilities: Gas,
Electric, Cable, Water $_____
Food $_____
Car Payment $_____
Gasoline $_____
Car Insurance $_____
Subtotal $_____

Insurance: Life, Health $_____
Medical $_____
Travel/Entertain. $_____
Clothing $_____
Repairs: Car, Home $_____
Education $_____
Other $_____

Subtotal $_____

Total Surplus/(Deficit) $_____

Do you expect any major changes in your income or expenses?

_____

Do you plan to make any large purchases in the next three years?

_____

ASSET TEMPERATURE

CASH/CASH EQUIVALENTS   **CURRENT VALUE**

Bank Checking
Bank Savings
Money Markets/CDs
Other

                TOTAL:

INVESTMENT ASSETS: **CURRENT VALUE**   **COST**

Individual Stocks
Individual Bonds
Mutual Funds
Stock Options
Limited Partnerships
Real Estate (not residence)
Business Interests
Education Savings/529 Plans
Annuities
Life Insurance (Cash Value)
Other

                TOTAL:

RETIREMENT: **CURRENT VALUE**

401(k), 403(b)
Profit Sharing
IRA (Traditional)
Roth IRA
Other

                TOTAL:

PERSONAL EFFECTS: **CURRENT VALUE**
DEBT AMOUNT

Residence   _____

Auto(s)   _____

Personal Effects   _____

Collections   _____

Credit Card Balance(s)   _____

Life Insurance (face amount)   _____

Other   _____

TOTAL: _____

TOTAL ALL CATEGORIES   _____

TOTAL NET WORTH   _____

APPENDIX 2

Rule of 72 Simple Calculation
8% Rate of Return Compounded

START	$100.00
END OF YEAR ONE	$108.00
END OF YEAR TWO	$116.64
END OF YEAR THREE	$125.97
END OF YEAR FOUR	$136.05
END OF YEAR FIVE	$146.93
END OF YEAR SIX	$158.69
END OF YEAR SEVEN	$171.38
END OF YEAR EIGHT	$185.09
END OF YEAR NINE	$199.90

APPENDIX 3

Rule of 72 Calculation
8% with money added at end of each year

End	Start	Interest	Addition	
START OF YEAR ONE	100.00	8.00	120.00	228.00
YEAR TWO	228.00	18.24	120.00	366.24
YEAR THREE	366.24	29.30	120.00	515.54
YEAR FOUR	515.54	41.24	120.00	676.78
YEAR FIVE	676.78	54.14	120.00	850.92
YEAR SIX	850.92	68.08	120.00	1039.00
YEAR SEVEN	1039.00	83.12	120.00	1,242.12
YEAR EIGHT	1,242.12	99.37	120.00	1,461.49
YEAR NINE	1,461.49	116.92	120.00	1,698.41
TOTALS	**100.00**	**518.41**	**1,080.00**	**1,698.41**

CPSIA information can be obtained at www.ICGtesting.com
Printed in the USA
LVOW02*1922011015

456563LV00001B/1/P